Helion Library of the Great War
Volume 2

THE
ADVANCE FROM MONS
1914

The Experiences of a German Infantry Officer

Walter Bloem

Captain, 12th Brandenburg Grenadiers

Translated from the German by
G C Wynne

With a Foreword by
Brig-General Sir James E Edmonds
CB, CMG, RE (ret.), *p.s.c.*

Compiler of the Official History of the War, France and Belgium

Helion & Company Ltd

Dedicated to the memory of my Regiment, Grenadierregiment Prinz Carl von Preußen (2. Brand.) Nr.12

Helion & Company Limited
26 Willow Road
Solihull
West Midlands
B91 1UE
England
Tel. 0121 705 3393
Fax 0121 711 4075
Email: publishing@helion.co.uk
Website: http://www.helion.co.uk

Published by Helion & Company Limited 2004

Designed and typeset by Helion & Company Ltd, Solihull, West Midlands
Cover designed by Bookcraft Limited, Stroud, Gloucestershire
Printed by The Cromwell Press, Trowbridge, Wiltshire

Originally published by Grethlein, Leipzig 1916
Original English edition published by Peter Davies Ltd, London 1930
This newly-typeset edition © Helion & Company Limited 2004

ISBN 1 874622 57 4

British Library Cataloguing-in-Publication Data.
A catalogue record for this book is available from the British Library.

For details of other military history titles published by Helion & Company contact the above address, or visit our website: http://www.helion.co.uk.

We always welcome receiving book proposals from prospective authors.

Contents

Publishers' Note

Whilst this particular book by Walter Bloem may be familiar to some readers, published as it was in an English edition by Peter Davies Limited in 1930, it is much less frequently known that the author wrote two further volumes of his Great War war experiences, to form a trilogy. *Sturmsignal* and *Das Ganze Halt* were published in 1918 and 1934 respectively. It is our intention to translate both of these works into English for the first time, to provide a unique inside view of the German army from 1914 until 1918. In 1940, the author's detailed history of his regiment's participation in the war was published in Berlin.

To provide some background to the author's experiences, it was felt that some brief details of his regiment might prove useful to readers.

Regimental notes

The regiment's full title was 'Grenadier-Regiment Prinz Carl von Preußen (2. Brandenburgisches) Nr. 12'. It was also given the nickname the "Kolonialregiment" due to its service in China 1900, and German South-West Africa 1904-06.

Formed on 1 July 1813, it saw service in many of the notable engagements of the later Napoleonic wars, or 'War of Liberation' as the Prussians termed it, including Groß Görschen, Bautzen, the Katzbach and Leipzig in 1813, Laon and Paris in 1814, and Ligny in 1815. Between 1846 and 1849 it was used to quell disturbances in a number of German towns, including Posen, Berlin, Halle and Erfurt, as well fighting the Danes in Schleswig, before earning more laurels during the 1866 Seven Weeks' War against Austria, and the 1870/71 campaign in France, during which it lost heavily at the battles of Spicheren and Vionville.

With its men hailing from Brandenburg, the Regiment was garrisoned at Frankfurt-an-der-Oder from 1881 until its disbanding in 1919.

One final interesting point to note is that during the 1914 campaign (and later in some cases on the Russian front) German regiments carried their colours into battle, furled and cased when on the march, and on the fly when going into action. At Bellot, on 4 September 1914, Leutnant Gräser of the 2nd Battalion greatly distinguished himself by waving the colours aloft as he rode into action - returning, miraculously, unscathed on that particular day! Within the space of twelve months, such actions on the Western Front seemed unthinkable, unimaginable even.

Bibliography

Readers wishing to read about the author's regiment and its part in the Great War in more detail are advised to consult the following sources:

von Schönfeldt, Ernst *Das Grenadier-Regiment Prinz Carl von Preußen (2. Brandenburgisches) Nr.12 im Weltkriege* (Oldenburg: Stalling, 1924: volume 103 in the series *Erinnerungsblätter Preußen*)

von Schönfeldt, Ernst *Verlustlisten des Grenadier-Regiments Prinz Carl von Preußen (2. Brandenburgisches) Nr.12* (Parchim: Gerlach, 1933)

Bloem, Walter *Das Grenadier-Regiment Prinz Carl von Preußen (2. Brandenburgisches) Nr. 12* (Berlin: Bernard & Graefe, 1940: volume 48 in the series *Deutsche Tat im Weltkrieg*)

Following the wholesale destruction of the old Imperial army's records in the destruction and diaspora of the Second World War, the voluminous regimental and other unit histories, published literally in their thousands by a generation eager to remember their comrades' sacrifice, remain today an unrivalled yet often ignored and poorly-utilised source.

Foreword

When compiling in 1921 the bibliography for Volume I of the Official History of the War, I included *Vormarsch*, by Walter Bloem, summarising it as "One of the most graphic and dramatic accounts of the war yet written. The author is a well-known German novelist, who was serving as a reserve captain in the 12th Brandenburg Grenadiers (III Corps of Kluck's Army). He gives the story of his experiences from the outbreak of war to the Aisne, where he was wounded on Chivres spur." Nine years later I still hold the same opinion of Herr Bloem's book.

I made a mental note in 1919 when I first read it – it was published in 1916 – that if no one anticipated me I would divert myself in my old age by translating it. This task has now been ably performed by my former colleague in writing the Official History, Captain G C Wynne, who fought as a regimental officer at Mons and Le Cateau, and was therefore a witness of many of the events to which the book refers.

In *Vormarsch* one has a unique record of the feelings of a combatant and of one trained to put them on paper; for Herr Bloem, before 1914, was the author of three novels on the war of 1870–1, a translation of one of which, *Das eiserne Jahr*, was published in English early in 1914. He is obviously a careful observer, with a photographic memory, and he wrote immediately after the events, during convalescence after the wound he received at the battle of the Aisne. His book, therefore, records his impressions before time had blurred them. Some of the scenes, for instance the attack of the British 12th Infantry Brigade on the 13th September 1914,[1] are so truly and vividly depicted that I gave translations of them in the Official History, feeling that they could not be bettered. The scene after the battle of Mons, which has been presented on the cinema, will remain for all time a record of the defeat of General-Colonel von Kluck by General Sir Horace Smith-Dorrien. The battalion commander coming out of the darkness of the night lays his hands on Bloem's shoulders, saying, "You are now my only support," and tells him that practically all the officers of the regiment are casualties. "And the men?" Bloem asks, and receives the reply, "The battalion is all to pieces – my splendid battalion." The author comments:

> A bad defeat, there could be no gainsaying it: in our first battle we had been
> badly beaten, and by the English – by the English we had so laughed at a few
> hours before.

Unfortunately, Bloem says very little about Le Cateau – the policy of ignoring this second defeat of Kluck by Smith-Dorrien and the aimless wanderings of the 5th Division to which Bloem belonged, was in force in Germany in 1916. In the morning he tells us the troops with which he was marching were caught in column on the road by a British battery, and there was "an almost panic-like uneasiness." For the rest, he only says, "We heard heavy gun-fire on our right for the whole day." There is no doubt he must have heard it. But what about the left, where the

1   See p. 110

6th Division (III Corps) endeavoured to envelop Smith-Dorrien's right and was checked by gunfire?

At the battle of the Marne the III Corps, which was commanded by General von Lochow, with Colonel von Seeckt as his Chief of Staff, again achieved nothing, spending the 7th and 8th September marching back from beyond the Marne to the right (Ourcq) flank. Only on the last day, the 9th, was the 5th Division sent against the British, but before it came in contact with them it was stopped and ordered to march north in the general retirement.

By the end of the battle of the Marne Bloem's battalion had nevertheless suffered so many casualties that it was reduced to two composite companies, and the men were absolutely worn out. He describes himself as he saw himself in a mirror:

> Lean as a skeleton, my skin covered with a regular crust of dust and sweat, my cheeks sunk in, my hair long and much greyer, my chin and jaw smothered with an untidy, greyish beard: so that was me!

The retreat to the Seine and the battle of the Marne, as will be seen, were a test of marching, discipline, and shooting rather than of fighting, and, better trained, the Allies won.

General Sir Horace Smith-Dorrien, the hero of Mons and Le Cateau, who first broke Kluck's onslaught on the Allied left flank, and foiled the envelopment which was the German Great General Staff's receipt for victory, should have written this Foreword. I had promised Captain Wynne to ask him to do so, but the very morning that I learnt his temporary address in England came the news of his fatal accident. Born and trained soldier as he was, he felt greatly the responsibility of fighting both at Mons and Le Cateau, and it always cheered him to know from German sources that he had done the right thing, and that the effects of his resistance had been so far-reaching. About 1 pm, during the battle of Le Cateau, he asked that a General Staff officer of the 4th Division should be sent to his headquarters to report the situation and receive orders. Major-General Snow sent me. On my arrival I saw that General Smith-Dorrien was obviously perturbed. He said to me at once, "Jimmy Grierson having died, I am sent out here without time to collect even a kit, still less to make myself fully acquainted with the situation, and I have had to make two great decisions. When I arrived before Mons the C-in-C told me to give battle on the line of the Condé Canal,' and when I asked whether this meant the offensive or the defensive, he told me to obey orders. That fellow … said to me this morning, 'If you stand to fight there will be another Sedan.'" I could only reply, "Please, don't let that worry you; we all feel that you have done the only possible thing." Indeed, had he not decided to stand with his 3rd and 5th Divisions the fate at least of the 4th Division, sent up by GHQ without signal company, cavalry, cyclists, or engineers, would have been sealed.

Herr Bloem's book will bring back the feelings of those great days to those who were of them, and will give others some idea of the stout enemy with whom the little BEF had to deal.

J.E. EDMONDS.
26th August 1930 (The Anniversary of Le Cateau.)

Diary of Main Events of the Campaign on the Western Front in 1914

August 1st: France, Belgium, and Germany order general mobilisation.

    2nd: Hostilities commence on French frontier. German troops enter Luxembourg. German ultimatum to Belgium.

    3rd: Germany declares war on France. England orders general mobilisation.

    4th: Germany declares war on Belgium. Hostilities commence on Belgian frontier. England declares war on Germany.

    6th: Battles of the Frontier begin.

    7th: Liège occupied by the Germans.

    14th–20th: Battle of Lorraine (Morhange and Sarrebourg).

    16th: Landing of the BEF in France completed.

    20th: Germans occupy Brussels.

    22nd: Battles of Charleroi and the Ardennes (including Virton).

    23rd: BATTLE OF MONS.

    24th: Retreat of the Allied Armies becomes general.

    25th: Fall of Namur.

    26th: BATTLE OF LE CATEAU.

    27th: Capitulation of Longwy.

    29th–30th: Battle of Guise (or St Quentin). Evacuation of Arras. Fall of Sedan.

    30th: Laon, La Fère, and Roye occupied by the Germans.

    31st: Amiens entered by German forces.

September 1st: Soissons occupied by the Germans.

    3rd: Reims occupied by the Germans.

    4th–12th: Battle of Lorraine (Grand Couronné, Nancy).

    5th: End of the retreat of the Allied Armies. Battle of the Ourcq. German forces reach Claye (10 miles from Paris).

    6th: Capitulation of Maubeuge.

    6th–9th: BATTLE OF THE MARNE.

    10th: Antwerp occupied by the Germans.

    12th–21st: BATTLE OF THE AISNE.

    12th: Capitulation of Lille.

    13th: Soissons, Compiègne and Amiens reoccupied.

    14th: Germans evacuate Reims.

    22nd–26th: Battle of Picardy (Noyon, Péronne, Bapaume).

    27th–October 10th: Battle of Artois (Lens, La Bassée, Armentières, Messines, Hazebrouck). Capitulation of Antwerp.

October 12th: Zeebrugge and Ostende occupied by German forces.

    19th–November 22nd: First Battle of Ypres. Battle of the Yser.

December 20th: First Battle of Champagne begins.

Map

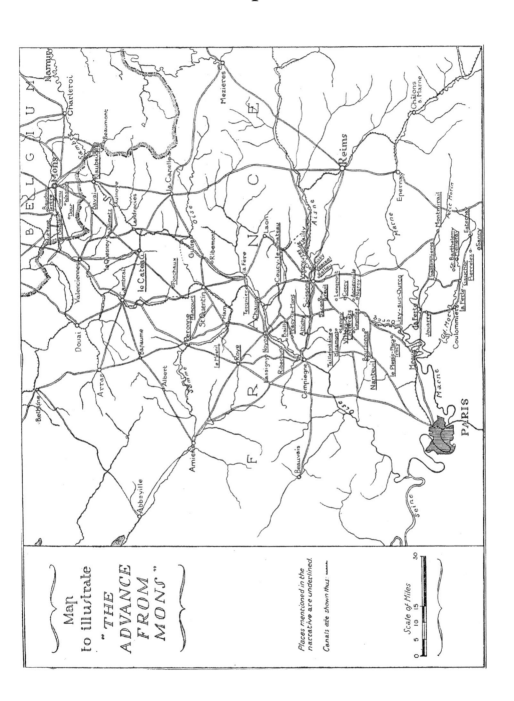

Map to illustrate "THE ADVANCE FROM MONS"

Places mentioned in the narrative are underlined.

Canals are shown thus:

Scale of Miles

0 5 10 15 30

Chapter One

Prelude

The three novels, based on the Franco-Prussian war of 1870, that I began in the spring of 1909, occupied the greater part of my thought and time until they were completed in the summer of 1913. My only other work was in connection with the Theatre Royal of Stuttgart from the spring of 1911 onwards as stage-manager and dramatic critic, my two plays *Volk wider Volk* and *Die Schmiede der Zukunft* being the outcome of this occupation.

The war novels finished I looked round for fresh inspiration, and my mind turned to the Alsace-Lorraine problem as their natural sequel. Taking advantage of a spell of leave from the theatre, I paid a prolonged visit to Alsace in the spring of 1914, and it was while sifting my impressions in the peaceful surroundings of St Odilien and embodying them in the first chapter of my new novel, *Das verlorene Vaterland*, that I determined on a complete change in my own life. I realised that the burden of carrying on two professions simultaneously had been too much for me, both mentally and physically, and that I could continue no longer, so I decided to resign all my commitments with the Stuttgart Theatre, to give up my house, store all my household goods, and then to go forth, about September, freed from all drudgery, into the great world with just my wife, my son and daughter already in their teens, and my writing. My wife and I would be able to enjoy the few remaining years of our youth in freedom together, and make the most of our children while they were still with us.

One duty remained to be fulfilled before our departure. The regiment in which I was a captain of the reserve would expect me to do another annual training with it, and so, on June 15th, I left for Frankfurt-on-Oder for four weeks of drill and military exercises. After that I should feel free to enjoy the reward I was promising myself for many years of hard and constant work. On June 10th, my forty-sixth birthday, although a year over the age-limit, I therefore put on my uniform once more.

During this training period the murder at Sarajevo took place. For a couple of days the effects flashed alarmingly, like summer-lightning, across the political heavens, and then the storm appeared to pass away, though while it lasted the talk among us officers was of nothing but an approaching war. However, this too gradually ceased, and when on July 14th I said goodbye to my friends, not one of us even in our innermost thoughts, let alone our spoken ones, imagined that in a comparatively few days we should all be meeting again in the barracks.

I went back to Stuttgart to my wife and family. Another six weeks to be devoted to the completion of *Das Verlorene Vaterland*, already half written, and then the planned flight away into the world. Then life would at last be wonderful, wonderful as a dream, free of all worldly cares, absolutely and entirely free.

Chapter Two

The Storm Breaks

So engrossed was I in my work during the days after my return home that I did not notice the course of world-affairs nor feel the muffled shocks that were already undermining the foundations of our social life. My visit to Alsace had exceeded my expectation in the quantity of material collected, and the plan that had formed in my mind during those weeks, at first mistily but gradually becoming clearer and more tangible, of a series of novels that would depict and bring home to the understanding of the victors of 1870 the condition of Alsace in the new German Empire, now began to take shape on paper, whilst all the time outside the world-storm was gathering. I worked in that short period with such enthusiasm and so cut off from the outer world, other than an occasional glance at the newspaper, that no hint of the great rumblings in the political firmament penetrated my home, and we were still quite ignorant of coming events when on Thursday, July 30th, we went to Hohenlinden to visit a newly married couple. Here I met Professor Franz Waterstradt, an instructor at the Wurtemburg Agricultural College near by and one of the best friends I had made in recent years. In the afternoon, while the ladies and children went for a walk in the park and gardens, the men of the party went for a ride by bridle paths through the woods and across the uplands of this lovely part of Wurtemburg. It was a perfect summer day, with the wonderful sunlit colourings of the trees and the standing corn intensified by the background of mountains all round, and yet an atmosphere of war seemed to fill the air, and our conversation turned almost exclusively to Waterstradt's favourite hobby, the mobilisation of the agricultural resources of the country. This fervent patriot explained his great scheme to us. Just as our military preparations had been worked out to the minutest detail in the event of war, so too, he thought, should the question of the nation's food supply be thoroughly examined and its control safeguarded by a comprehensive scheme of labour organisation, to include every available pair of arms and every wagon in the country. What a loss to Germany was this man, in a few months to go to his long sleep on French soil, when later all his ideas materialised.

It was dusk when we returned to the station, and there the stationmaster told us of strange and amazing rumours he had heard. Our homeward journey was full of anxious thoughts, though they seemed incredible.

The following morning we scanned the headlines of the newspaper, trembling with excitement, and then stood aghast, staring at each other. There it was in black and white – the rumours were true. Filled with blank astonishment I hunted up the official pamphlet giving the requirements of a mounted officer on mobilisation, and made out from it a list of a hundred-and-one odds and ends. All that morning I worked almost feverishly at my novel – only a few chapters were left to finish it – and after lunch we went into the town and shopped continuously for two hours. The town itself had not yet been noticeably shaken out of its usual lethargy, but everywhere in the streets and shops were men with lists of things to buy in their hands, like myself, and many of their womenfolk were already in tears.

In the evening we packed my regulation officer's trunk and kit bag, and then the four of us sat under the lamp in the library, as was our usual custom, not knowing what to think or say about it all. Again and again I thought, "Was it really possible?" So long and so hard had been our struggle to make good, and so close, almost in our grasp, the prize – two years of travel. The autumn we were going to spend in Capri, the winter in Egypt, the spring probably in Greece, and so on; we looked into a future full of sunshine, and were expecting to start in only a few days' time. And now, what of this other future? As I meditated on these dreams, so long planned, so much desired and so near fulfilment, and yet now in these evening hours so near to fading cloudlike back into dreamland, I almost wept. Only when I pulled myself together did I feel all at once a powerful hand, strong as steel, leading me on and pointing ahead. A sudden confidence both in myself and the future entered into me as never before, and it was undoubtedly a foretaste of those miraculous self-revelations I was to experience in the bitter days of battle to come.

Such was the chaotic state of my feelings, full of anxiety and yet with a great enthusiasm gradually and secretly awakening within me, as I sat with my much-loved family on the eve of the world struggle.

Although a state of war had been declared in Germany, and Russia was mobilising, there still lurked in some small corner of the heart a grain of hope. It had happened before, and each time the storm had blown over and all had gone on as usual: the same work in the same circumscribed little area of one's existence, the varying experiences, joys and sorrows, in one's own narrow little sphere of influence. Perhaps it would happen again, and in a fortnight's time we should all be sitting on the Grande Marina at Capri, laughing at the anxious moments we endured that evening. And with these thoughts we went to bed and to sleep, while outside in the big world the fate of nations lay in the balance.

The next morning, Saturday, found me again at my desk, writing as one possessed. I was astonished at myself, at the flow of ideas and the rapidity with which they covered the paper. It was as if subconsciously I knew it to be the last opportunity to complete my novel, this final gift to leave behind for the support of my family in a future full of dark forebodings. But by midday, although only a few more pages were left to write, all power of expression left me. The feeling that the hour for action had struck and that the time for story telling was past completely overcame me. I got up and left the work unfinished. After lunch we again went shopping, buying, buying, buying. Several shops were sold out. A map-case was not obtainable, and I was fortunate to get the last pair of Zeiss field glasses – a splendid pair they were too. What experiences many of these purchases were to share with me – two electric torches, a small collapsible hurricane-lamp, an aluminium drinking-mug, a knife with every imaginable contrivance – to have a history of its own – and so on.

About six pm a friend, Lieutenant Justi of the Grenadiers, bursting with youth and energy, met us in the street. He had been the pilot when Karl Rosner and I made our first balloon trip, one icy winter night the previous February, from Stuttgart to Metz. He came up beaming and almost hoarse with excitement: "The order to mobilise is out. I've just had it on the telephone from Berlin. I'm off tonight to my aerodrome." And with that he hurried on leaving us with little doubt as to the future. And while our young boy in his childish innocence was shouting for joy at the prospect of all the excitement ahead, my wife and I looked for a brief moment deep into each other's eyes and I realised, come what might, how indissolubly united we were for all time and eternity. Our self-control failed us. The tear season had begun – already they were everywhere. Eta, our brown-haired little daughter, was silent and gave no vent to her feelings, though her pale little face was filled with a look of terror.

We went on our way as if in a dream, buying and still buying, at the same time waiting for the moment when all these people around us would know the news as we did. And in a very short time a white paper was being pushed into every hand, into ours as well, and on it in large and ineffaceable letters just the one word: "Mobilise."

A crowd of young men came across the square from the palace after cheering the King,[1] and went on to the house of the young Archduke Albrecht. He came out on to the balcony and made a fine soldierly speech, brief and to the point. And then followed mighty shouts of hurrah for the Kaiser and Empire. No doubt of it now – the inconceivable had happened.

There was still much to do. Although not due to rejoin my regiment till the third day of mobilisation I felt I couldn't stay idle, and decided to join up at once, leaving the next morning, Sunday. We finished packing, labelled each of the four things, my trunk, my brown kitbag, and the two boxes of saddlery for my two horses, with the special red labels, "War luggage. Immediate," and then we all four, father, mother, and children, sat together in the library for the last time. And when I thought of the morrow, when my life would be taken up in the clutches of that remorseless monster, War, I realised as never before, looking round at my family, how intensely happy and fortunate I'd been in my life and how truly grateful I should be.

It was the end of a stage, a milestone in our lives. I fetched a couple of bottles of the sparkling wine we used to drink so merrily when we could afford it to celebrate the end of one of my books or plays. The glasses clinked together, and we held hands as we drank. Extraordinary! It felt as if tomorrow we were all off together to the land of the sun instead of – where?

In how many thousands of homes were families sitting together that same evening, like us, celebrating, strangely enough, the great farewell. Nevertheless even now it all seemed too mad to happen. Those in power must surely see what a mighty flood of misery and suffering they were letting loose on humanity, and find some other solution than this impossible and incredible war. In any case, whether it came or not, it had been the cause, in these few and blessed evening hours, of opening our eyes to show us how rich we had been, how rich we were, in all things worth having.

1 The King of Wurtemburg

Chapter Three

Leaving Home

The next day, Sunday, August 2nd, was the first day of mobilisation, and we all started off for the station on foot, the luggage having gone on ahead.

My home was a rented one, and I had cared little for it, but as I closed the front door behind me for good I realised for the first time what a large piece both it and the town itself had gradually eaten out of my heart. Up there in my study I had put in the three best years' work of my life, and here, in this town, I had looked for the first time on Success. I had, as it were, fought the battle of life here and won through, and now, at six-and-forty with my hair already flecked with grey, I was leaving the scene of my triumphs for another battlefield, for the sternest fight of all.

The bells were ringing and crowds were thronging into the churches. At the corner of Palace Street and King Street was a red placard with a crowd around it: "Libau is being bombarded by our fleet. Violent encounters between German and Russian cavalry."

No longer just mobilisation: this meant bloodshed. Now there could be no withdrawal. It was too late. War was a certainty. My wife glanced into my eyes and in that second I saw that she too had understood. She was to give up to her country her husband and all she had of home and happiness. The great sacrifice had begun. My little Eta too, always a silent child, keeping her deeper emotions locked away within her, said nothing, but leaning her brown head against my shoulder, her eyes filled with tears. Dear child, I shall never forget those tears – your silent, priceless gift of love.

At the station all was confusion; but after much delay the Berlin Express eventually came in. The last kisses, the rush to the carriage-window as the train started, then farther and farther away, there they stood, my three loved ones, waving and weeping. To you, my wife, how much I had still to say and to offer. So long together and yet it seemed that only now were we just beginning to understand how much we meant to one another. And as the train gathered speed, the ever-memorable picture gradually swam in the mist of tears in my eyes. My wife – my children – *auf Wiedersehen, auf Wiedersehen.*

Chapter Four

Joining The Regiment

We were due in Berlin at 9 pm but did not arrive till six next morning, and it was four o'clock that afternoon before I reached the barracks in Frankfurt. As I got out of the cab, Lieutenant Maron came up to greet me.

"Hallo, Bloem! Who'd have thought this when we parted two weeks ago?"

"Yes, who indeed."

"You're to command B Company."

This news astonished me. I did not expect to have a company, but Maron told me its commander, Gebhard, had been sent to form a new company of the Reserve Regiment. I went along at once to the office of the 1st Battalion, and there met Lieutenant Stumpff, the adjutant, a strapping, red-cheeked youngster, who took me in to the battalion[1] commander, Major von Kleist. Everywhere the same warm-hearted welcome, the spirit of a big, happy family ready to pull together in all weathers.

"Well, Bloem, you'll have your hands full the next few days," he said. "Both your subalterns, Lieutenant von der Osten and Lieutenant Grabert, are away on duty bringing in the reservists. You'll have to do all the mobilisation work of the company yourself. Just you and your sergeant major, Ahlert. But he's a real good man, as you know."

Soon afterwards I was in the office of "my" company with "my" sergeant major: the father and the mother of the company. Ahlert was a smart, strong fellow, still young, and every inch a soldier. We shook hands – a firm grasp to confirm our spoken words that we would have complete confidence in each other and work together as good friends. We kept to our promise.

"Will you speak to the company a minute, sir? About fifty reservists have come in already."

I agreed. Ahlert paraded them, and I went across to my future comrades-in-arms with an exuberant song of joy within me.

"Company – Right-dress." Ahlert, with the firm, measured step and confidence of the well-trained, long-service non-commissioned officer, went to the right flank, corrected the dressing, then – "Eyes-front," and in a moment he was standing stiff and straight as a statue in front of me.

"Company present, sir. Fourteen NCO's and one hundred and sixty-two men."

All eyes turned upon me. I could feel them examining me, testing me; could they trust me or not? And silently my heart vowed loyalty to each of these hundred and seventy-six strangers.

---

1 A German Infantry Regiment in 1914 had three battalions, each of four companies, subdivided again into three sections. The war strength of a company was 250 NCO's and men.

"Good-day to you, B Company."

"Good day, sir," came the reply, all together, almost a shout, a battle cry. The four walls of the barrack-square re-echoed it. I ordered them to come round in a circle and made them my first speech, the first of many. I told them it was the proudest moment of my life to be standing there in command of B Company of our famous Twelfth Grenadier Regiment "From east to west," I went on, "enemies are advancing on us to break up our beloved country. It is up to each one of us to fulfil the highest duty of German manhood, to defend his home, his wife and his children. It will be a great disappointment to you that your former company-commander, Captain Gebhard, has been taken for other duty, and that instead you are to be led into battle by an officer of the reserve, whom none of you know. I fully appreciate your feelings in that respect, and I have as yet no right to expect your confidence and trust. Nevertheless I can promise you that it will be my constant aim in the days to come to earn it. More I cannot say. Grenadiers know what their duty is when they are called to arms, and I will only add one more request, that we all stand together through thick and thin, fair weather or foul. Let that be a solemn promise, taken here and now, and let it be confirmed by three cheers for His Majesty our Emperor and Commander. Hip! Hip! Hurrah!"

Back again to the company office, and there I discussed with Ahlert the programme of work for the following days. The regiment was to be ready to march out by the evening of the 7th, so that only three days were available for all the business of mobilisation, but a glance at Ahlert's calm, determined face, as if saying, "That will be all right," assured me, and I for my part would not fail in assisting him.

Grenadier Weise, detailed to be my servant, reported to me – an honest, reliable face. He put away my two boxes of saddlery in the barrack room and took my trunk and kit bag to my quarters in the town. Here I heard that thirty thousand refugees from East Prussia, fleeing from the Russian invasion, were coming to the town and accommodation had to be provided for them; and also that German troops had crossed the Belgian frontier, irrespective, of Belgian neutrality. I wondered what England would say to this last bit of news. That morning, too, there had been a remarkable sitting in the Reichstag.

A message from the Kaiser had been read: there were to be no political parties for the time being, only one all-German party: the Socialist-Democrats had passed all the war-credits without a murmur. The nation was in fact one immense united brotherhood.

Chapter Five

Mobilisation

The world suddenly seemed to become a different place. It appeared to contain nothing but men – and horses. Wherever one looked, endless streams of men in the streets, men from the factories, men from the towns and men from the country, workmen in their overalls, clerks in their black coats, foresters and peasants in their coarse cloth suits, all marching together, all singing together, all coming to the barracks, and the great iron gates opened and swallowed them up. Once inside, they became transformed – their different appearances vanished. Bit by bit they stripped off their everyday coverings and clothed themselves all to the selfsame pattern, the selfsame colour, the dull service grey of modern war – not without many a laugh at the reservist bellies around which no belt would meet, and at great square skulls on which the martial headgear sat perched like a student's cap. Then there were the horses – snorting, rearing, and stamping everywhere. Sturdy cart-horses, powerful vanners, light hacks from gentlemen's stables, prancing thoroughbreds, steeple-chasers, browns, blacks, chestnuts, bays, all sorts and colours, excited by the change from their daily routine, the railway journey, this great gathering of their kind, by the cracking of many whips and the shouting – all sweat and commotion.

The regimental commander, Colonel von Reuter, rode across the square. He greeted me in the serious, almost gloomy way he had.

"I congratulate you, sir," I said, "on having the honour to take into battle the same regiment at the head of which your father was killed at Spicheren."[1] A gleam of ecstasy lit up his bronzed features, and I felt that he wished no finer death himself, for which all honour to him. Then more handshakings, more greetings on all sides, particularly with the other officers of my battalion, my future comrades-in-arms: Spiegel, the commander of A Company, with his black and white medal-ribbon gained in the East African rebellion of 1905-06, a hardy veteran whose previous war experience we all envied: Count Reventlow, calm and amicable, in spite of his sarcasm, and full of energy, who had commanded C Company for some years; and Goerdt, an officer of the reserve like myself, commander of D. In the afternoon Sergeant Schüler, to command No. 3 Section of my company, arrived, a slim, well-educated fellow, a bank clerk in Berlin.

That evening I saw from Sir Edward Grey's speech in the House of Commons that England was against us – another enemy. In spite of the so-called "isolation policy" we had not expected all these enemies. Later in the evening came the news that England had declared war on us. When I went to bed that one thought kept running through my head.

---

1 Spicheren was fought on August 5th, 1870 during the Franco-Prussian War

Chapter Six

Parading The Regiment

Three days later, on the evening of the 7th, the regiment, fully mobilised, was paraded. My company was now up to establishment, a quarter of a thousand all told. The brand-new leather of the boots and equipment creaked and crackled, and only the figure 12 in vivid red on the helmet-fronts relieved the drab grey monotony of the general turnout. The three battalions of the regiment formed three sides of a square, and in the middle was Colonel von Reuter. He made a speech. What he said I don't remember, perhaps I never knew, but all those three thousand around him understood; for it was not an individual speaking, but all of us speaking – Germany speaking. And then three cheers from the Twelfth Grenadiers, cheers such as the barrack walls had never echoed before nor since.

We were to entrain early the next morning. In the meantime my two subalterns returned: Lieutenant von der Osten I already knew, a tall, well set-up fellow and a first-class professional soldier, and Lieutenant Grabert, in peace-time a member of the Geographical section of the General Staff, a thick-set, robust youth, with a dry and rather crude sense of humour. They had had no trouble with the reservists, and as they had been travelling about a good deal I asked them what was the general feeling of the country towards the war. In reply they gave an account of scenes so stirring and so full of intense patriotism as to be almost beyond belief; it was the picture of a nation rising up immense in its unity, gigantic in its strength, to complete its self-expression, to fulfil its destiny. My brain reeled at the greatness and grandeur of the moment; I saved myself in my work.

Chapter Seven

To The Front

Five a.m., the hour of departure. A rosy haze in the east veiled a cloudless dawn. "B Company – Fall in! Officers – draw swords!" Mine came smartly out of its scabbard; the only time I was to draw it in the whole campaign – quite useless, that beautiful, long, arrogant blade.

"Slope – arms! Form – fours! Right! Quick – march!" I went to the head of my company as it took its place in the column, my heart filled with more pride than I ever thought it possessed. We were off.

The hour of departure had been kept secret and Frankfurt did not expect its Grenadiers to leave so early. The streets were empty, only here and there frightened women's faces peeped through the curtained windows. The companies marched through the booking-hall on to the platform alongside a train of tremendous length. Where were we going, east or west? The engine was facing west, but that meant nothing, perhaps just to mislead spies. The order was given, and in a moment the train was filled to bursting-point with its living cargo. Many of the men wanted to decorate the carriages with inscriptions "To Paris, " "To London," etc, but Major von Kleist forbade it. "Wait till we come back as victors," he said.

The public were not allowed on the platform except for one young and frail little lady, the wife of the battalion adjutant, married the previous day. She restrained her emotions most admirably, typical of her Prussian upbringing. The carriage doors were banged. The stationmaster brought his hand to his red cap in salute, the whistle blew, one solitary white handkerchief waved, and the train moved off. How many of us were to return? How many were to remain – out there?

Once away from the town the wide spaces of Germany opened up before us and I felt a terrible homesickness. Far away to the southwest my family would be still asleep; and in silence I thought of them and of this sudden astounding change in my own life. Just before reaching Berlin we were switched 'off through the southern suburbs on to the main line – to the west. As soon as this new direction was quite definite there was a general rejoicing. For some undefinable reason the very thought of Russia gave one a shudder. Not only that, but as the intention we imagined was to act on the defensive in the east, while the mass of our armed strength overran our enemies in the west in one great onslaught, it was there that we wished to be.

We bought the morning papers at a wayside station and read, amazed, of the experiences of those of our troops already across the Belgian frontier – of priests, armed, at the head of marauding bands of Belgian civilians, committing every kind of atrocity, and putting the deeds of 1870 into the shade; of treacherous ambushes on patrols, and sentries found later with eyes pierced and tongues cut off, of poisoned wells and other horrors. Such was the first breath of war, full of venom, that, as it were, blew in our faces as we rolled on towards it.

The journey seemed never-ending, so many and so long were the delays; we did not reach Düsseldorf till the following evening, Sunday. The men were almost visibly fattening with the masses of chocolate and sandwiches poured into their carriages at every stop. On the way we had read of the fall of Liège: a giant gun of Krupp, with shells as big as a man, had blown the defences of the Belgian fortress to matchwood. That and more and more stories of revolting cruelties on our troops by Belgian civilians filled the papers. As we passed through the great industrial towns of Westphalia we were agreeably surprised at the great enthusiasm shown by all the workers there for the war. Flags flying everywhere, and cheers far more whole-hearted than we'd expected, all along the line. The big junctions were filled with train-loads of guns, countless masses of guns and motor cars of all descriptions – private cars, commercial vans, motor lorries – come, as the inscriptions on them showed, from all parts of Germany. And the sight of all this brought home vividly to our imaginations the terrible chaos into which our wonderfully ordered country, running like clockwork, had been plunged in so few days. When would the mess be untangled, sorted out again – when indeed?

That evening, as the sun was sinking among a mass of heavy, crimson clouds away on the western horizon, we crossed the Rhine. As the train came above the middle of the river a mighty yell arose from the whole length of it, and then began the great chorus, that song of our fathers:

Zum Rhein, zum Rhein, zum deutschen Rhein!
Wer will des Stromes Hüter sein?
Lieb Vaterland, magst ruhig sein,
Fest steht and treu die Wacht am Rhein!

Was it real or was I living in a dream, in a fairy tale, in some heroic epic of the past? For four years I had put all my heart and soul into describing the very experiences now taking place. My novels had suddenly become my own living present, my words had become my own deeds – an incredible, surely an unprecedented situation for a novelist. And as I realised the meaning of it all, my heart overflowed with that great joy of fulfilment, with the fullness of living.

Chapter Eight

Into Belgium

It was pitch dark by the time we arrived at Eisdorf, an outlandish village station, which, as we could see by the light of the arc lamps, had now become one of the main railheads of the concentration zone. We detrained and marched to our billets, feeling exactly as if we were on manoeuvres. After two days and a night in the train the men were thankful to leave it, and most of them complained of stomachaches as a natural result of the superabundance of food so lovingly showered on them throughout the journey.

Early the next morning we began the first march in piping heat. Although only about ten miles, the older reservists groaned under the burden of their heavy packs, some collapsing by the roadside. We billeted that evening in the village of Oberzier. Away to the west dull, muffled thuds, boom … boom … boom – guns perhaps at Liège, perhaps only our training-camp at Elsenborn, but in any case the sound gave me a strange quickening of the pulse. The following day the manoeuvre feeling continued, especially when during the morning we practised deployment and an attack in extended order over the fields, and then formed up on the road again and marched on.

By degrees I was learning more about the men of my company, those that had any outstanding characteristics or special occupations, more particularly my two orderlies, Lance-Corporals Sauermann and Niestrawski; the former, a lean but well-built Brandenburgian, quietly efficient; the latter, a cunning, witty Pole with plenty of cheek and chatter. Then there was Pohlenz, my bugler, a sturdy, unconventional Berliner with a home-made cigarette eternally in the corner of his mouth; and Willy Weise, who at his own request had become my groom, and handed over the care of my personal belongings to a rather sleepy Grenadier, by name Zock; Mussigbrodt was my horse-holder on the march. These six, then, I ordered to form my "staff," to share my quarters with me, and to remain close at hand as much as possible, instructions which they carried out to the letter, and they were to become my most faithful and almost inseparable companions.

That evening I found a map of Europe in the village school near our billets, and gave my company a lecture on the general situation as far as I knew it, and never have I had a keener and more grateful audience. The German soldier, unlike the Russian *moujik* who blindly does what he is told, wants to understand what he is doing and think it over for himself. He should be given the credit of this and have things explained to him accordingly as much as possible; there is then no limit to his response.

After that, a few hours' rest. We officers were sitting together in a shady orchard drinking beer when suddenly there was a shout: "Aeroplane over." True enough there it was above our heads. We knew our own should have a black cross under the wings, but looking through my glasses I could see no cross, neither did my companions. Then it must be an enemy. I was about to give the order to the men near by to fire at it, when suddenly from the next garden shots rang out, and then there was no holding the men – they all fired at it. We got hold of rifles ourselves and fired at it. It flew on, but the next day came a severe reprimand. One of our airmen, ran the message, had been fired at, and in future no aeroplane was to be fired at without orders from an officer. That, then, was our first great deed in the world war, shooting at one of our own airmen.

The next day, August 12th, brought us to Weisweiler. In the evening Lieutenant Gräser, a subaltern of A Company, asked me to dine with him. He had a splendid billet with a most worthy old lady who had a charming niece staying with her. There, in a most attractive up-to-date bathroom, I had my first bath since Frankfurt, and the luxury of if was unforgettable. After a meal we all four went to the market square where our band was playing, and had coffee outside a restaurant. The band struck up *Es liegt ein Krone im tiefen Rhein*. Gräser had a splendid voice and we both sang to it.

Where was this war? I thought, as I went back to my own quarters outside the village; so far it had been simply manoeuvres. And then suddenly a long column of open lorries came past, and in them sat the lightly wounded from Liège, with their blood-drenched bandages still upon them. I gazed at them with mixed feelings – astonishment, anxiety, and also envy; they had received their baptism of fire, the first ordeal was over for them, they knew what it was.

Another very hot day's march through Stolberg, Weiden, Haaren to Forst, an industrial suburb of Aix-la-Chapelle. I was billeted here with a Catholic priest and fed like a fighting-cock. On wishing me goodnight he begged me to kneel, although I was not of his faith, and he gave me the blessing of his Church – a downright good man, a most saintly Christian and a good German citizen. That was my last billet on German soil. The following morning, equipped with his blessing, I set off towards the Belgian frontier at the head of my company, on my good horse, Alfred, so christened after the young hero of my trilogy of novels.

At Weisshaus, near Lontzen, the field-cookers came up and we had our midday meal from them for the first time. O beloved cookers, how could we have got on without you? Without you the world war would have been an impossibility.

Drowsily digesting, we crossed the frontier without realising, and therefore celebrating, that historic moment, and later in the afternoon reached our first billets in the enemy's country, the little village of Henri-Chapelle. The stories in the newspapers as well as our orders on the subject made us particularly cautious. The men entered the houses in which they were to be billeted for the night with loaded rifles and fixed bayonets, and the local inhabitants were asked to drink from the wells before any of the water was used. My own quarters were in the house of a doctor then serving in the Belgian Army, but the caretaker welcomed us in fluent German and asked my subalterns to dinner as well. He served up some excellent beef-filets and the champagne flowed freely. Just like manoeuvres, still.

And then I went up to my bedroom, the doctor's own room. After five years of happy married life, his wife, as I learnt, had died a year since, and the perfectly charming and exquisite Louis Seize bedroom furniture must have been the gift of most devoted and well-to-do parents to an idolised daughter. The bed, as broad as a billiard table, was as soft and comfortable as a dream of love, and I crept in between the silken sheets with feelings that beggar description. And this was my first night in the enemy's country! Through the open window I could see far away on the distant horizon the blood-red flickerings of blazing fires reflected against the sky.

Chapter Nine

Advancing Through Belgium

Saturday. Already a week had gone by since we marched out of barracks at Frankfurt. A week of manoeuvres. But now all that was at an end, and with a rough jerk we were suddenly to find ourselves among all the abominable horrors of war. No sooner had we begun the day's march than we saw the first traces of the monster we were going to meet. Every fifty yards the Belgians had dug trenches across the road. They had since been filled in, of course, but the marks were there of this childish, futile effort to hold up our advance. Also the fine trees all along on either side had been felled across the road by these deluded peasants; obstacles that our engineers must have just laughed at. And there, by the roadside, lay the first dead horse we'd seen, its black carcass all swollen up, and from its mouth hung an unpleasant mass of congealed blood, teeming with flies.

The road now ran along a high ridge, and we overlooked the hilly country at the northeastern end of the province of Liège. Belgium, a free, bright, and happy country, full of delightful memories for me during many visits, and now – the enemy's country. Incredible! To our right lay the prosperous village of Clermont, apparently unchanged, but in front, on the crest of a rise in the road, was the outline of another village with quite a different aspect. The church tower seemed to have no spire, an unusual thing in these parts, and in front of it was a queer jagged row of houses; at a distance it all looked strangely empty and most mysterious. Just before reaching it there was a long halt, during which the artillery came forward and took their places in battle-order in the column. First came the light batteries of Regiment No. 54, my company being detailed as an escort and put in between the two brigades;[1] then the heavy artillery clattered by, drawn by enormous horses, snorting and champing as they passed.

Looking ahead and looking back the column stretched out of sight in both directions like some gigantic snake threading its way through the countryside. The division was now complete with all arms up to war strength – a mighty stream of men of which I and my company formed a very small part.

The column moved on again and into the mysterious village, called Battice on the map. As we approached, the reason for its strange aspect became apparent; it was burnt out, completely gutted. Marching along the streets one could see through the frameless window-openings into the interior of the rooms with their roasted remnants of iron bedsteads and furnishings, and broken bits of household utensils of every kind lay scattered about the street. Except for dogs and cats, scavenging among the ruins, all sign of life had been extinguished by the fire. In the market square stood the roofless, spireless church.

---

1 A German Field Artillery regiment in 1914 had two battalions, subdivided into three batteries each of three sections of two guns.

And as I passed on through this devastated village, riding at the head of my field-grey cohort with the guns rattling along in front of me, I was staggered by this first, horrible vision of the red-hot passion of war, and I said to myself: This simply can't be true. You are imagining it all. You are reading some mediæval, heroic saga of barbaric times, and this procession of hideous pictures is being conjured up by your too vivid imagination as the story unfolds. It is inconceivable that you, a homely, peace-loving novelist, should be sitting here on a war-horse, dressed in all the panoply of war – you, who, although you do occasionally write of battle, murder, and sudden death in your books, in real life take up even the caterpillars you meet on the road and put them carefully on a leaf in the hedge to save them from being run over and trampled on. Undoubtedly it's all a dream, a nightmare, nothing more.

Nevertheless, the ghostly and ghastly procession of pictures did not cease, and we had scarcely left the village behind us when – ping! – ping! – ping! from the edge of a small wood to the right, and two or three bullets whistled past behind me and just over the heads of my company.

In a flash I awoke from my dreaming. "Lieutenant Grabert, line the ditch on your right with your section. – Open fire on the edge of the wood. – Two rounds each man!"

The shots rang out like a volley. The whole company wanted to line the ditch and fire too. "Stay on the road, the rest of the company, and keep moving on slowly," I shouted. A few figures could be seen running off through the undergrowth, and some of Grabert's men seemed about to give chase. "No, Grabert, stop them; they'll never catch the brutes. Join in the column again." And the march continued.

Monstrous thought, to have been hit, perhaps killed, by one of those bullets fired into the column by a few civilians. A few bitter words among the men on the subject, all seeing red for a moment in our anger, and then we calmed down. In silence the giant snake kept wriggling on along the endless road unceasingly. From time to time I rode back alongside my company and noticed with astonishment that no one was falling out, that today there appeared to be no weaklings. They were all plodding silently on, mile after mile, the sun blazing down upon them, the sweat trickling in streams down their faces, and still they all kept on. Was it the excitement that kept them going, the sight of so many things they'd never seen before, or was it the thought of the reported tortures awaiting them at the hands of marauding bands of armed civilians at night, if they dropped out of the column?

Ahead of us another village. This one apparently unharmed; and then suddenly a great column of blackest smoke, then another, then a third, mounted up above the roofs near the street, all close together. The black cloud curled, twisted, eddied this way and that, great tongues of red flame shooting up through it and spreading out in all directions. In a few minutes the whole village was in flames and we had to march on through it. It was like marching through Hell. The scorching glow almost stifled us. Cattle bellowed desperately in a blazing barn; hens, their wings and feathers singed away, rushed about the street demented; and what was that lying huddled by a wall? Two dead men in peasant's smocks. At a crossroad stood a section of the Brandenburg Guard Regiment that formed the advanced guard of the Division that day, and near them a few engineers were shovelling earth back into a freshly dug grave. I asked them for the solution of this riddle, the cause of all this welter and chaos. "Sir," came the answer, "as our leading cavalry patrol was riding through the village, three of the Hussars were shot dead in the street. The other three Hussars dismounted, entered the house where the shots had come from, and there found two peasants with rifles still in their hands. They seized them, and they've been shot, and orders were given to burn the village to the ground." A suitable revenge and a just punishment.

In the next village we came to, a whole street of houses lay in ruins, not gutted by fire, but knocked flat as if by a colossal blow from the northern side. Beyond, on top of a green hill, pitted with shell-holes, the black, white, and red flag flew triumphantly. The map gave me the clue to this second riddle of the day. That green hill was Fort Barchon, one of the outer works of Liège, that had held out to the last, and the marks of the firing of our heavy guns battering against it were visible on all sides, including this street of ruins.

"Halt! Two hours' rest," ran a message passed along down the column. The giant snake lay down and stretched itself out by the roadside. We all seemed to adapt ourselves to the new conditions with amazing rapidity. Sergeant-Major Ahlert came up to me with the news that he had discovered two pigs in a shed; should he take them and have them slaughtered?

"All right, give me a requisition form and I'll sign it."

Ahlert smiled. "The people have all left."

"Well then, leave the form on a table in one of the rooms."

"But the house is on fire, sir."

"Well, don't then. War is war."

Elberling, one of the two company butchers, said he had found a good place to kill the pigs in, but the owner was still in the house and wouldn't allow it. "Will you speak to him, sir?"

I found a fat and valiant Belgian innkeeper, obstinately defiant and in a sullen temper. I said to him, "Look here, monsieur, no nonsense, please!" and clanked the steel end of my scabbard noisily enough on the flagstones of the inn for him to take notice of it. With sunken head he turned and led the way, my two butchers following with the mistrusting, squealing pigs, and then for the first time in my forty-six years I witnessed, with all the naïve astonishment of a townsman, the spectacle of the killing and cutting up of a pig.

With fabulous speed those two sturdy Grenadiers, Liebsch and Elberling, converted the unhappy animals into a heap of human food, and a few moments later it was being thrown into the field-cooker to add to the evening meal. We had, we were told, still a long march ahead of us before night.

Beyond Wandre, we suddenly came to the Meuse valley, lying below us at our feet and stretching away into the distance. In a succession of sharp, twisting bends, the road descends steeply to the river-level, and as we crossed it the regimental band struck up to help us along. Passing on through the manufacturing suburb of Herstol all the windows and street corners were crowded with gangs of factory hands who had stopped work and now stared at us, their eyes full of hate.

We continued on to the north-west, this everlasting march, and whenever I trotted to and fro alongside my weary company to cheer them up and urge them on I was met with the question, coming at me almost reproachfully all along the column, "How much farther, captain?" And I could only tell them that God only knew. It was beginning to get dusk. Through a gap in some heavy clouds to the west we noticed a shining silver apparition; an airship hanging apparently motionless up in the sky, miles away. To our right a couple of heavy siege batteries was in position, facing Liège, that lay away to the left; it appeared that two of its southwestern forts were still holding out and the fighting still in progress, though we couldn't hear a sound.

The remainder of the march, in the failing light and eventually in darkness, was through an interminable succession of villages with a mass of turnings and crossroads. Marching behind artillery is no pleasure, even in peacetime and in daylight, but in war and in the dark it is a great trial. After every block and check of the column, the guns trot on and pick up the unit in front, leaving the heavy-footed infantry to follow on and keep touch as best they can. Consequently I and my two cyclist orderlies had to spend our time keeping up communication with the artillery often three or four hundred yards in front through this difficult district with so many crossroads and turnings. I must confess that as I trotted to and fro through these dark streets, with excited groups of civilians at every corner, I felt distinctly nervous, the more so, perhaps, because of the experiences of that day, and I had my loaded revolver ready in my hand all the time.

This most uncomfortable method of travelling lasted several hours till well into the night, and yet on this day, in spite of having covered twenty-eight miles, not one of my lads fell out, not a single one. The thought of falling into the hands of the Walloons was worse than sore feet.

About midnight we arrived at the village of Glons, and my company was allotted two villas for the night's rest – a rest of four hours only. The smaller villa I gave to Grabert's section, and took the other two sections on to the larger one. In the square and the streets was a seething mass of troops and a deafening hubbub and din. We knocked at the door, rang the bell, and knocked again, and no answer. Locked and bolted. The axe was the only way in, and so it was that these hundred and eighty dog-tired, hungry men, after a day such as they'd never known before, burst through into the well-cared-for and charmingly decorated home of some respectable citizen. The orders were to take care of all private property and make only reasonable use of it, but what was more natural than that these men, who had to sleep on the floor, without even straw, should lay their hands on everything soft or warm in the house, for use either as mattress or pillow? I stopped twenty, thirty men who were upsetting everything in these pretty rooms, but by now I realised definitely, I knew with no further shadow of doubt that I was at war.

After four hours of confused slumber I awoke. Outside in the garden Elberling was slaughtering a bullock; this, too, was a novel spectacle for me. We did what we could to tidy up the rooms again, and then the field-cooker appeared with coffee. When the time came to fall in I vowed that never again would the company sleep inside a nice house – they would bivouac outside it. I can honestly say that I had kept good order, but by the morning I was worn out with the effort.

While waiting for the order to move off I had a chat with two villagers standing by. They said: "The rich people, sir, those with plenty of money, have all gone off. Before they left they wanted to turn us poor people into a kind of police force. We were to look after their goods and chattels, their villas and gardens, while they were away – ha, ha, ha! We laughed in their faces. Why didn't they stay themselves as we had to? As soon as you're gone, then, possibly we too shall have a look at their beautiful houses – from the inside. Only out of curiosity of course, *vous comprenez*, m'sieur!" And their greedy eyes looked across at the comfortable little villa colony over the way.

So this was the spirit, the attitude of mind that the war had brought in its wake. Could it possibly be good for them or anyone else this loosening of the bonds of common honesty, this lack of any form of respect? To these people nothing was sacred any more.

At last: "Quick – march! March at ease!" We were off again. It was Sunday, a sunny Sunday, but today no one was thinking about going to church. The villagers stood about in anxious groups in front of their houses, but they didn't seem to worry, and throughout that day's march not a shot came from houses or hedgerow. I noticed, too, that whenever I spoke to any of the villagers, they now answered in a language that was more familiar to me, more reminiscent of my frequent visits to Belgium, and then it struck me that, of course, we had passed through the Walloon half of the country, and were now in that part of it that spoke the Flemish dialect. That expression of hatred and suspicion on every face had gone, and when questioned they replied fearlessly and at their ease, laughing whenever I attempted to make myself better understood in their own dialect. Major von Kleist, the battalion commander, noticing my frequent conversations with the local inhabitants, told me I was to act in future as his interpreter.

The day's march took us through cheerful, gently undulating country, and neither the villages nor a single house showed any trace of war. The German barbarians had had no cause to give way to their innate propensity to fire and murder. It was a shorter march, and by two in the afternoon we were in our new quarters, the village of Bloer, that lies on the low side of the main road, at the edge of a large bog, a tangle of swamp, thicket, and trees, and an ideal place for an ambush. Major von Kleist, therefore, gave orders that a man, or if no man was available, a woman, be taken from every household as a hostage and kept together under a guard overnight. He asked me to see to this.

I had very nice quarters, an inn by the roadside with a small shop attached. The proprietress, who spoke French and German equally fluently, received us in a most resigned manner. I decided that the hostages, who were collected together with as little commotion as possible and treated with every consideration, should pass the night in the coffee-room, and they made a queer picture, this medley of people huddled together in the room, guarded by two of my Grenadiers with fixed bayonets. Naturally the incident had caused tremendous excitement in the village. The wives and children of the hostages had come along to the inn with them, sobbing, beseeching, and praying to Heaven that I wouldn't shoot their menfolk, and I had the greatest difficulty in calming them. Throughout all the confusion, the proprietress kept perfectly calm and dignified, and although the tears were running down her cheeks as her own husband and his brother were among the hostages, she was quite friendly towards us, cooked for us, baked bread for us, kept up her work in the shop, acted as mediator in any difficulty, and did everything possible to calm the troubled waters in the village – a typical Teutonic woman, full of pluck and vitality.

The next day's march was without incident. It took us along the old Roman road that leads from Aix-la-Chapelle through Maastrecht and Louvain to Brussels, which we should have been on all the time since Aix-la-Chapelle but for the fact that we had to go round the Limburg appendix of Holland, whereas the road cuts straight across it. I and my "staff" were now quite accustomed to each other, and had settled down admirably to the new conditions. As soon as we reached our night's quarters I, as father of the company, was given the best room with the bed, giving up any unnecessary blankets and pillows to my two orderlies, Sauermann and Niestrawski, the bugler, Pohlenz, and Zock, my servant, who all slept next door; my two grooms slept near the horses.

An early start was ordered for the following day, and when at 3 am I went to battalion headquarters to report my company ready to march, I found the major and the adjutant in the middle of a very excellent breakfast. They gave me the latest news. Ahead two streams crossed our road, between us and Tirlemont, flowing north; they join up about Budingen, and thence, as the River Gette, flow on through Diest. Our march on Tirlemont could be very effectively opposed by a determined enemy operating against our flank from the northwest, and since reconnaissance patrols had reported the presence of enemy cavalry and cyclist troops in the neighbourhood, the Division had orders to capture this sector of the Gette. At last an encounter with the enemy was in sight.

It was still dark when the battalion moved off – and at every beat of one's throbbing heart the thought repeated itself, today we were going into battle, our first battle. After passing through St Trond we left the Roman road and moved off to the northwest in order to deploy for the attack against the line of the Gette. The deployment took place in daylight and by 7 am was completed, my company being along an embankment and awaiting the order to attack. To our left, on the front of the neighbouring division, the artillery fired the first shots, breaking the silence of this sunny August morning. While giving my orders and seeing them carried out I had no time to think of my own feelings, but I was aware of a slight uneasiness, a kind of strained suspense, as if faced by something that was going to put me to the test. Added to that, a colossal urge forwards, on, on, and not to wait; let whatever is to happen happen soon. And my Grenadiers, what were their feelings? Their faces were filled with a look of tense expectation, everywhere the same burning desire; now at last, after all this foot-slogging, to grapple with the enemy, to catch him by the throat!

Finally came the order to advance. I led the way on my horse, the company following in company-column not yet extended in battle-formation. We started off as smartly and correctly as if on a parade-ground, but this didn't last long; for very soon a miserable fight began, not with the enemy, of which there was still no sign, but with the tricks and fancies of a perfectly crazy bit of country, a mad confusion of small copses, meadows, and farms criss-crossed by ditches, hedges, and barbed-wire fences in all directions. In order to keep our proper direction we had to go straight ahead regardless of all these obstacles, and after following a lane a short distance I put my horse at a big hedge and ditch into what seemed at a rather casual glance to be a nice, soft meadow below on the far side. We jumped and then suddenly – crash – squash – and I was up to my hips, horse and all, in a great squelching bog. My faithful "staff" ran up, and at once sank up to their waists in the morass. I scrambled off the wildly plunging Alfred, and after a panting fight we eventually got on to terra-firma, and then hauled the trembling, sweating Alfred out of his mud-bath. We were smothered up to our waists in a coal-black, sticky slime, and Alfred was covered with it from head to foot, the contents of my saddle-wallets being completely spoilt.

However, what did it matter; forward, on, on. Luckily the sun was now shining, hot as an oven, and dried, superficially at least, our dripping clothes. I made the best I could of a bad business and joined in the roars of laughter of my company when their captain reappeared looking like the driver of a muck-cart.

But where was the enemy? Where were his shells and bullets that might well have been knocking us to pieces in all this mess-up? Incomprehensible; not a shot, not a shell anywhere, even the gunfire on our left had stopped.

Scratched all over by thorns and barbed-wire, many with their clothes badly torn, all of us wet through both from outside with slush and from inside with sweat, we trudged on through this labyrinth. Adjutants, orderlies, staff officers rushed hither and thither trying to straighten out the confusion or find their own units again. After a couple of hours they succeeded, and the division was assembled once more near the village of Budingen and moved up on to the high ground, this being the out-of-the-world and sparsely inhabited district known as the Hageland. There we had a three-hour halt, but no midday meal; the eagerly awaited cookers never turned up, and at 5 pm we moved on again through this deserted rolling upland, uphill, downhill, uphill, and downhill, through occasional sleepy, empty villages. The men, utterly exhausted with fatigue, hunger, thirst, and sore feet, were almost at the end of their tether, and it was hard work to cheer them up and keep them going. I constantly had to ride up and down the line, reproaching them or joking with them, anything to get their gradually sinking noses up in the air again. And still onwards, onwards.

It was beginning to get dusk, when, suddenly, rifle-fire ahead of us. The column halted, the guns moved away into position on our right flank and opened fire. A fight! The 1st Battalion was to be in reserve and waited in the narrow side-street of a village close by. Meanwhile it had got quite dark, and then the northern sky was gradually lit up, getting more vivid and glaring every moment until finally a high, bright pillar of flame rose up into the sky. Our guns had set on fire the village of Capellen. The artillery and rifle fire gradually died down, and then the news slowly leaked through; the enemy had evacuated the village. Now back into the column again, another mile or so of marching, or rather shuffling along, and at midnight the battalion arrived in the village of Suerbempede, thoroughly done up and starving.

And that was our first battle-day.

In the inky darkness we were allotted two barns and a comfortable, homely-looking house for the night. I allotted the house to von der Osten and his section, and for myself took the other two sections to the barns, one each. They crowded into them and lay down just as they were; a horrible lodging after such a day. It was nearly 1 am when I got back to the house with Sauermann and Niestrawski, and I could scarcely drag my legs up the front steps I was so tired. As the door opened to my knock, an unexpected sight appeared; a venerable old man, with a few snow-white hairs, in the threadbare vestments of a priest, a flickering candle in one hand,

and carrying under the other arm a bottle and two glasses. In a kind, though slightly awkward manner, he invited me to come into his house. The heavy boots of my Grenadiers stamping about, upstairs and downstairs, were making a terrible din all through the house, but the old man remained unperturbed. He put the candle on the floor and poured, with rather a shaky hand, the gleaming red wine into the glasses, offered me one and held the other towards me: "Your good health, captain, and welcome to the simple home of a poor parish priest."

We had heard enough stories about Catholic priests leading their parishioners in treacherous ambushes, poisoning drinks, and so on, so I was not surprised when Sauermann and Niestrawski (even though the latter was himself a Catholic) caught hold of both of my arms and whispered: "Don't drink, sir, the rascal is sure to have put something in the wine."

I looked at the rascal carefully once more. He? No, never.

"Monsieur le Curé," I said, "my friends here warn me not to drink your wine; they say you may have poisoned it. But I will rely on my judgment of human character. Your very good health!" and I clinked my glass on his and drank it down in one long, thirsty pull.

"Oh! captain; I, a poor parish priest, poison you? Never, sir, I am a Christian like you." And in a truly Christian manner did the pious father treat us. My Grenadiers had already spread themselves all over the house, but he made no complaint. Only one thing he asked, and that was that I should have a look at his refugees.

"At who?" I asked.

"My poor people, captain. Some of my parishioners who have come to me for safety in fear of the invasion."

"But we do no harm to anyone who doesn't harm us," I replied, as the old man led the way to his kitchen. I opened the door; a many-voiced cry of terror greeted me; two dozen terrified pairs of eyes stared at me despairingly. The whole kitchen was crammed full of people of all ages, women, children, and old men, among them two ladies of a better class and well dressed. I had difficulty in convincing them that not one hair of their heads would be touched. They had come to their parish priest to escape the "barbarians." I ridiculed the idea.

"Has any one of you ever seen a German soldier commit any infamous act?"

"No, sir, oh no! But all the world says that you leave no one alive."

"Indeed! Well, now you can see for yourselves to the contrary."

I was implored to tell my men not to harm them.

"That would be a nice thing to tell my men. They will harm no one who does not treacherously fire on them."

After that I sat with the old priest in his study and had supper, an excellent omelette made by himself, washed down with good wine. We spoke of the difficult, terrible times that had suddenly come over our lovely world, and the priest said he had foreseen it all for a long time; mankind, sinking deeper and deeper in sin and luxurious living, was fast degenerating, and such a punishment as this from Heaven was bitterly needed. And I thought, as I looked at the touching poverty around me, of his life of unselfish devotion among these plain, worm-eaten bits of common-deal furniture, these much-read, worn-out books, and how helplessly he must have struggled against the insolently rich and, to his mind, sinful inhabitants of this wealthy district. And now the war had come, and he regarded it as a judgment of

God, as a modern version of the Flood, to wash away all sins, and he bowed down before it in humble resignation.

The next day, August 19th, was the worst yet. It seemed as if the still blazing village of Capellen had enraged and maddened the whole neighbourhood. Though actually the result of a skirmish with the enemy, the peasants appeared to regard it as an unmerited and deliberate Hunnish act. We had scarcely got out of the village before we were fired at from every hedge and from every window. Consequently columns of smoke and flame soon belched up into the sky, far and near; men were dragged out of the houses, and any found with a rifle were given short shrift. Others who were only suspected had their hands tied behind their backs with washing-cords, and were driven along with the column until later they could be tried by court-martial.

From the noise of the shots there were probably stragglers in uniform behind the hedges, sniping at us, as well as civilians with sporting rifles, but any thought of pursuit was out of the question, as this district, full of quickset hedges and copses, was a paradise for guerilla warfare. A volley into the hedge or wood where the shots came from, then on! If any were caught, then they got what they deserved.

The roadside was now littered more freely with articles of Belgian uniform and equipment – hats, short dark blue coats, light blue trousers, packs, and so on – but no rifles. We did not know until now that the Belgian infantry soldier carried a suit of civilian clothing in his pack.

Suddenly, halt! Mounted orderlies and staff officers hurried hither and thither. In front of us the villages of Butsel and Hoogbutsel were held by the enemy. The regiment was to attack. I dismounted; the company extended out into the fields and I went to my position twenty yards in front of the centre of my line, my "staff" close behind me. We advanced across a soppy meadow, and then rifle-fire opened from the edge of the village in front, and there was a noise like the twittering of a lot of swallows about my ears.

"Listen, lads! what's that strange tschiu-tschiu-tschiu going on all round us?"

"That's bullets, sir," said Sauermann, quite at his ease.

"Oh! so that's bullets! Well, they don't seem to hit us, and so we'll go on." And on we went until we came to the edge of the village. For the last hundred yards the twittering had ceased. The village was empty. The sections were closed in and we passed through the village. Beyond was another green meadow and then another village – Hoogbutsel. More rifle-shots, more twittering of swallows. To our right, two hundred yards ahead, the Fusilier battalion was extended, lying down. It opened a heavy fire on the village edge, and then began to advance in short rushes. Soon the twittering stopped again. We moved slowly on and saw a number of men in dark and light blue uniforms being assembled by the Fusilier battalion and taken to the rear. The first prisoners we'd seen.

We reached the village without casualties again, and found to our astonishment German troops already occupying the southern side of it, part of the IX Corps that had been marching parallel with us on our left. Attacked from the flank, the enemy had cleared out.

Farther on, in a field near Bankersem, we had a long rest, and, thank goodness, the cookers were there. Another short march in the boiling midday sun, when a message arrived: "Enemy advancing from direction of Louvain in front; on the right the villages of Pellenberg and Cortenberg held by the enemy."

As we, company commanders, were riding back after getting orders from the battalion commander, a few bullets from the high ground to the right hit the road – pitsch, pitsch – between the horses' legs. A sunken lane enabled me to trot on ahead of the company to see the line of advance, while von der Osten's section extended to right and left of the lane. Bullets were humming past, when suddenly there was a sharp report close behind me; von der Osten had shot a partridge with his revolver.

Now I dismounted and, climbing up the bank, saw rising ground in front with a row of house-tops appearing over the ridge – Cortenberg village. Osten was already moving his section up to the ridge; now they were coming under fire, they began to double and then disappeared over the top.

"Lieutenant Grabert," I shouted back, "halt here with your section and wait for orders." I went on up to the ridge and there, two hundred yards in front, Osten was in position, firing hard at the edge of the village. The enemy's fire was coming from the boundary hedges of the gardens and from the attic-rooms of the houses, and there were rusty red as well as thin grey puffs of smoke, showing that civilians as well as soldiers were firing at us. I signalled to Grabert to come on, and a few moments later his section was on the ridge. I jumped up and went forward with them, and in three long rushes we had reached and reinforced Osten's line, out of breath, and a whole chorus of swallows twittering all about us. Damn it! this was more like business.

"Open fire, Grabert! Aim just below the roofs." And soon a hail of bullets was rattling against the houses, tiles, and brick-dust flying. Still the dull cracks of sporting rifles, showing that civilians were also engaged, and through my Zeiss glasses I could clearly see how our fire was gradually forcing the enemy to leave the garden hedges and double back, man by man, into the houses, and nearly every one was a civilian. One of them ran across the open towards the cover of a wood. "Don't let him escape, lads!" And he didn't; he lay there dead in mid-field.

The enemy's fire died down, and on the flank, where C Company was attacking, it had completely ceased.

"B Company!" I shouted, "Forward – at the double." In one long spurt we got to within fifty yards of the garden hedges, lay down, and fired a final volley into them.

"Fix bayonets – charge!" Up again and on, as if doing a drill on the parade ground. The last defenders rushed across the gardens and disappeared among the houses. It was over. I called out to my subalterns: "Form up your sections for the advance on Pellenberg." We moved on. There, in the open field, lay a dead civilian, blood streaming from several wounds. I was on the point of extending out again for the attack on Pellenberg when a message came from the battalion: "A and D Companies have taken Pellenberg. B and C Companies form up and follow the regiment on the main road towards Louvain."

Just as we moved off there was a stampede of riderless horses on our right, two or three dozen coming towards us. "Catch them!" I called out, and half the company spread out, I with them, and we caught seven, mine a very handsome black mare, obviously belonging to a Belgian cavalry regiment, the lances still in the stirrup-straps. With out booty we marched on in good spirits, my Grenadiers in full song. Forgotten, those two weeks of endless marching in the sweltering heat and dust, for now we knew what it was; we had had our baptism of fire. What a curiously solemn expression that sounds, and yet in reality how commonplace and matter-of-fact it is. There in front is the enemy; he shoots at you, and you shoot back at him. No time to think of danger, or of the fear of being shot, one just shoots and perhaps kills without thinking that one may also be killed oneself.

The Fusilier battalion of our regiment was attacking Louvain. A few shells, a certain amount of rifle-fire, and the skirmishing lines, had reached the edge of the town. We had halted on a flat plateau overlooking it, and could see through the midday haze its towers and Gothic roofs and spires. The cookers came up and the captured horses were distributed, the black remaining in my possession and nicknamed by the men, Alfred the Belgian, a name it kept. A message arrived: "Louvain is ours. Continue the march."

After an hour we passed through one of its deserted suburbs, where a few Belgian priests, with Red Cross bands on their arms, came to meet us, very solemn and reserved. I described the place where I knew some wounded lay, and they promised to bring them in and attend to them. Unfortunately we did not go through the town itself, but skirted its southern side. Some Belgian soldiers came out to us with uplifted arms and were taken on in the column as prisoners. This was indeed an easy victory, and we went on our way singing merrily: "*O Deutschland hoch in Ehren*," and "*Es braust ein Ruf*."

The inhabitants stood in large groups at the street corners, their faces masking their thoughts, though a number of girls were laughing and winking at us. The road now lay on higher ground and, looking to our right over the tops of an avenue of elm trees, we had a good view of this beautiful town with its fine spires and towers shining gold in the afternoon sun. Six days later rebellion, street-fighting, and wholesale conflagrations were to rage here, but now it was a picture of peace, perfect peace.

It was beginning to get dark when we approached our billets in Berthem. Suddenly a message: "Enemy entrenched on the high ground to the west. Attack them."

We deployed into column of sections off the road towards the high ground and then extended out. A wood lay along the top of the hill and our artillery sent a few shells over us that burst exactly along the edge of the wood where the enemy were. That was sufficient; they bolted. We went back to the road. In front a pillar of flame shot up in the evening twilight, then another, three, five pillars of flame. Our village, our billets were on fire. After much delay, confusion, and exhaustion, the order finally came: "The battalion will bivouac at the western edge of the village, with outposts out towards Brussels."

We pitched our camp among the burning houses, near some gutted farm-buildings which would have made most comfortable night quarters. Our first war-bivouac! I lay down under my narrow shelter tent and was sound asleep in a second.

That was August 19th, the birthday of my far-away and beloved little daughter, and I had not remembered it, I hadn't even given it a thought.

We rose early, washed in the dew on the field, and marched away into another radiant summer morning. At midday we were to march into Brussels. Brussels –

the Belgian capital. It was fabulous, surely a dream. Was this whole war just a game, a kind of sport? Was this Belgian Army just a pack of hares?

We passed through Tervueren with its green parks, its fine railway station on our right and its magnificent castle on our left, and then along a wonderful avenue, the great arched corridor of trees that leads through the Forest of Soignies, in which we had a halt. All the time one felt that queer prickling sensation of victory, goading us on; in less than an hour we would be entering Brussels. Actually, however, we turned left-handed just before entering the town and marched through the southern suburbs, bivouacking that evening in a field near Ruysbroek. My company had to do outpost duty covering the battalion bivouac from the west; I posted the piquets and sentries and the evening passed as pleasantly as if on manoeuvres and the night in delightful summer peace.

The next morning our heavy baggage appeared for the first time. I opened my regulation trunk in a farmyard, and what pleasure to see everything lying there just as those dear hands had packed them at Stuttgart! And as I turned them over, such a fragrance of cleanliness and comfort, such a fragrance of home arose that hasty tears came to my eyes. My dear ones away back over there! No news for two weeks and no means of sending any back. The field-post brought nothing and took nothing, there was no bridge between us over the great gulf of the past two weeks.

Only a short march the following day. In the town of Hal there was an unexpected halt. Adjutants and mounted orderlies clattered over the cobbles. An enemy was said to be holding the ridge south-west of the town and a fight appeared probable. After a while more messages. No! again nothing. Really it was like having war administered to us in small homeopathic doses.

Inquisitive people gathered round us as we waited. A well-dressed lady approached our battalion commander, and taking from her bosom a rosette in the Belgian and English colours, handed it to him with a sweet smile. Major von Kleist quickly gathering together all he knew of the French language replied: "Madame, che crois, que vous – croyez – que che suis – ung Anglais – mais – che ne suis pas – ung Anglais – che suis – ung Allemang." Horror on the part of the lady and a hasty withdrawal.

An elderly, intelligent looking man came up to me and, pointing to the field-cooker which was just starting off and smoking, asked: "Please, sir, that is a gun to defend you against aeroplanes, isn't it?" "Yes, of course, monsieur – it's going to fire almost immediately – look, it's smoking already … "

Sergeant Schüler, the smart young clerk of Berlin, was surrounded by flirting femininity. The people of Hal, in fact, seemed to find no difficulty in overcoming the fact that we were not Englishmen; and the German atrocities consisted in a most harmless catching of twinkling eyes. That, at all events, is the only atrocity I myself have experienced, seen, or reliably heard about. The people treated us with real friendship. My company's billets were in a disused sugar factory, and here, at any rate, there was nothing to spoil. Out of use for some years, it was rapidly tumbling to pieces, but the inhabitants brought us a quantity of straw and made the big ruined sheds quite comfortable.

My two subalterns and I were quartered in the villa of a manufacturer. He welcomed us most amiably and introduced us to his charming wife who, in a rustling silk dress, led us three filthy fellows into her drawing-room and gave us coffee, liqueur brandy, and cigarettes. Our conversation was as if we were paying a visit among our own people, though the subjects were rather more serious.

"Why has your little Belgium offered this senseless and useless resistance to our overwhelming superiority?" I asked.

"You must think of our self-respect, captain," said Monsieur P, "and what the rest of the world would have thought of us if we had just let you pass through. But now we have done enough, I think, to preserve our honour, and we all hope that our gallant young King will make a reasonable peace with you."

"Do you know where your King is?"

"He is fighting with our splendid troops, who have retired behind the forts of Antwerp, and there I expect he will await your representatives to negotiate the peace."

"We also hope that may happen. The two countries have always been on such good terms."

"And hasn't our brave little army fought brilliantly, captain?" asked madame, her fine black eyes sparkling with patriotic enthusiasm.

"Most certainly, madame," I replied, with my tongue in my cheek. "They have fought like bull-dogs."

We got on splendidly together. I had a most luxurious bath, the first since Weisweiler – unadulterated, heavenly bliss – and in the evening we had a three-course dinner with champagne. Monsieur in his tail-coat, madame in a smart low-cut dress, and we in our war-garments, all brushed up and as tidy as we could make ourselves. The conversation was a mixed grill: a little bit of war, quite a lot of art, Rubens, Jordaens, Geefs, Meunier, Belgium's seaside resorts, Blankenberghe, my holiday reminiscences, and so on. I had to show them the photographs of my beloved family. My subalterns, whose conversational command of the French language was limited, drank, smoked, looked sympathetic when necessary, and smiled whenever madame showed her beautiful teeth. What a wonderful world it was, to be sure, and how easy to get on with one another, even with our enemies!

The following morning we set off again, now in a south-westerly direction. Distant artillery fire could be heard, but we ourselves marched in the most profound peace. We passed through Enghien, alongside an interminable park wall: historic memories of Napoleonic times came to one's mind. The heat became positively oppressive and the men began to get disheartened. These everlasting long marches day after day ... I shared out my last cigarettes and offered to carry one of the men's rifles: he seemed to be staggering a bit, and though the others jeered at his lack of backbone he gave in and let me take it. Soon I was carrying another as well, both slung across my chest, and even though on horseback it was quite enough. We halted at midday in a field somewhere for a rest. Suddenly an aeroplane appeared overhead. This time there was no doubt about it: the red, white, and blue rings under the wings could be seen with the naked eye. I told off two groups to fire at it, and soon everyone seemed to be firing at it. It turned back as if to return southward but too late: its nose turned down, it made several corkscrew turns, and then fell like a stone a mile or so away. Murmurs of satisfaction all round. A little later three Hussars came past and shouted out that they had found the aeroplane in a field farther on. "What about the pilot and observer?" I asked. "Both in bits, sir."

During the afternoon we arrived at Thoricourt. The heat had affected me, and feeling feverish I sank on to a large bed in my farmhouse billet. My "staff" attended to me as if I'd been a sick pet lamb, but only for a few hours, as my company was again on outposts and I had to ride round the piquets and have barriers put across the roads in front. Enemy cavalry were reported in the neighbourhood; English, so it was said. English? Good God! the very thought was enough to make one die with laughter.

The fact is that by this time the whole war seemed to have lost its true perspective for us. The serious aspect of it had almost faded away. It had become a joke, though a hard-working one. Nothing but march, march, march, to an extent never imagined by us. We had now done fourteen consecutive days without a single rest-day. It had apparently become a matter of beating the enemy with our legs, for he would not stand up to us. Where was he, anyhow? The Belgians were off the map, and the French and English, who had promised that unfortunate little country their protection, where were they? So far we hadn't seen a sign of them, and tomorrow, Sunday, we were, if all was well, to cross the French frontier.

We had outmarched our communications. Not once had the supply columns got up to us, and we had had to live on the country, fortunately a very well-stocked one, taking what we could find. Of coffee, meat, potatoes, and vegetables there was no lack – only bread, that failed us completely, and I now learnt for the first time what a vitally important part bread plays in the life of the working man. The Grenadiers began to grumble about the flour rations.

"Look here, lads, you get three warm meals a day; coffee and porridge in the morning, meat and vegetable soup at midday, and enough of it to tighten your bellies, and in the evening porridge again – how much more do you want?"

"We get no bread, sir."

"That's true, I get no bread myself either. There's flour in sackfuls but no time to bake it, and no yeast. All the same you've been able to fill yourselves every day."

"But we get no bread, sir, and without bread no man can carry on like this for long – anyway if he has to slog along twenty to thirty miles every day."

I shrugged my shoulders. "Children, we are at war. I am giving you all I can get."

"Having no bread is bad enough, sir, but having no post is ten times worse."

"I quite agree with you, children. I also don't know what's happening at home – but neither do they at home know what's happening to us, and they are ten times worse off than we are."

"Anyhow it shouldn't be so," grumbled my Grenadiers. "It's all wrong."

"Remember again, children, it's war, and very likely there is much worse still to come."

And there was, and soon too.

Chapter Ten

Mons

Sunday: the second since we crossed the Rhine. Reports coming back along the column seemed to confirm the fact that the English were in front of us. English soldiers? We knew what they looked like by the comic papers; short scarlet tunics with small caps set at an angle on their heads, or bearskins with the chin-strap under the lip instead of under the chin. There was much joking about this, and also about Bismarck's remark of sending the police to arrest the English Army.

The day, though overcast, was sweltering hot again. The sweat poured off the men's faces as they trudged on, and a big wood we marched through made the atmosphere even more stifling, rather than cooling us with its shade. The regiment was advanced guard, and after a march of some twelve miles halted in the village of Baudour. Hussar patrols, trotting past, reported the country free of the enemy for fifty miles ahead.[1] The cookers were brought up and we settled down to a comfortable midday rest. Scarcely had we finished our meal, when two Hussars, covered in blood, galloped up to us stating that the enemy was holding the line of the canal in front. A third Hussar limped along behind them, carrying a blood-stained saddle; his horse had been shot under him: "They are in the village just ahead."

I called to Ahlert: "Tell the company to hurry up with their meal. We shall probably be moving in a few minutes."

Almost at once despatch-riders, adjutants, motor-cyclists rushed past. Somehow we all felt in our bones that this time there was going to be real business. A signal from the adjutant; the Major wished to see the company commanders. "Mussigbrodt, bring my horse." In a moment we were gathered round our battalion commander.

"Maps out, gentlemen! The village of Tertre in front of us is held by the enemy: strength not yet known. The regiment will attack. The Fusilier battalion, supported by two batteries in position south of Baudour, will occupy Tertre railway station. We, the 1st Battalion, have orders to take the strip of wood west and southwest of Baudour – you will see it on the map, gentlemen – and clear any enemy out of it. We shall be supported by Wiskott's Battery. My orders, therefore, are as follows: The battalion will advance at once on the strip of wood, companies in the following order; B, A, C, D. B Company will send out half a section both to its right and left as flank-guards to the battalion. Any questions, gentlemen? No. Then please move off immediately."

I galloped back to my company. "Fall in!" I sent Sergeant Schüler with half his section to the right and the other half under Corporal Tettenborn to the left.

---

1 These patrols had probably gone out south-westwards towards Valenciennes and, therefore, past the left flank of the British Expeditionary Force that was advancing northwards from the Maubeuge-Bavai line. In that case their report would have been correct.

Tettenborn, a gallant and splendid soldier, I never saw again; he lies buried at the southern edge of Tertre village, one of the first of the regiment to be killed.

We marched off. The Fusilier battalion was extending out, its front line of skirmishers already under enemy fire from the direction of Tertre station,[2] a few bullets whistling over us too. Wiskott's Battery galloped past, and a few minutes later, as we turned off to the right towards the wood, the guns were already unlimbered alongside a factory-wall, their muzzles pointing at the wood. The battery commander was on the observation ladder looking through his glasses, and we had scarcely got past before they opened fire, the first shells whizzing just over our heads.

The battalion now deployed for the attack. My company was to clear the centre of the wood, crossing through it in a south-westerly direction; A Company was to clear the southern part, with C on its left moving on the north-west end of Tertre village; D in battalion reserve.

I now had only two sections in hand, and ordered Lieutenant von der Osten to take a group of his No. 1 Section to the railway embankment on our right, covering that flank and moving along it as far as its point of junction with the northern edge of the wood where he would regain touch with the company. The remainder of his section, under Sergeant Holder-Egger, was to extend and go through the wood, keeping the south-westerly direction: I would go with it. Lieutenant Grabert's No. 2 Section was to follow in support.

We struggled through a mass of dense undergrowth, and reached the farther edge with our faces and hands scratched all over, but otherwise met no opposition. Looking from here Tertre village was on our left, and from the noise of rifle-fire and bursting shells it was clear that heavy fighting had begun with a n enemy not to be so easily brushed aside. In front lay an extremely long, flat, marshy-looking meadow. Its left side was broken into by scattered buildings and sheds, and on the right a narrow strip of wood jutted out into it. At the far end, about 1500 yards straight ahead, were more scattered groups of buildings. Between the near and the far buildings a number of cows were peacefully grazing.

We had no sooner left the edge of the wood than a volley of bullets whistled past our noses and cracked into the trees behind. Five or six cries near me, five or six of my grey lads collapsed on the grass. Damn it! this was serious. The firing seemed at long range and half left.

"Forward!" I shouted, taking my place with three of my "staff" ten paces in front of the section leader, Holder-Egger, and the section in well-extended formation ten paces behind him again. Here we were, advancing as if on a parade ground. Huitt, huitt, srr, srr, srr! about our ears, away in front a sharp, rapid hammering sound, then a pause, then more rapid hammering – machine guns. Over to our left, about Tertre, the rifle and machine-gun fire was even more intense, the roar of guns and bursting shells increasing. A real battle this time!

---

2 Tertre was occupied by the 5th Divisional Cyclist Company and a few patrols of A Squadron 19th Hussars (5th Divisional Cavalry). They were supported by A Company of the 1st Royal West Kent Regiment in an advanced position at the crossroads south of the village.

We were approaching one of the scattered farm buildings in the meadow, and being the first I went in, and noticed at once a group of fine-looking horses, all saddled up. I turned to my "staff": "Get hold of the horses; but look out! Where there are horses there must be riders." I had scarcely spoken when a man appeared not five paces away from behind the horses – a man in a grey-brown uniform, no, in a grey-brown golfing suit with a flat-topped cloth cap. Could this be a soldier? Certainly not a French soldier, nor a Belgian, then he must be an English one. So that's how they dress now! All this flashed through my mind in the fraction of a second, and in the meantime the fellow had raised his arm, a sharp report, a wisp of smoke, and the whisk of a bullet passed my head. In the same second I had pulled out my loaded revolver and fired – peng! – missed too. He dodged behind the horses and I behind the buttress of a wall – my blasted revolver had jammed! I pulled the empty case out of the chamber: it ran free again. Then I peered round the side of the wall aiming, ready to fire. Yes, there he was, his long, thin face just behind a horse's tail looking at me, also along the sights of his revolver. We fired simultaneously, again missed by a hair s breadth, and then suddenly he rushed away with long strides into the meadow. Ten, twelve shots rang out and he fell dead on the grass. My staff had run round to the other side of the building to tackle him from behind: he had seen them and then took to his heels, but too late.[3]

"Holder-Egger, stay here with two men to hold the horses – hand them over to be taken back as soon as you can – mind you say they belong to B Company."

"Right, sir!"

"Come on, the remainder!" As we left the buildings and were extending out again, another shower of bullets came across the meadow and rattled against the walls and all about us. More cries, more men fell. In front a farm track on a slightly raised embankment crossed our direction.

"Line the bank in front," I ordered, and in a few short rushes we were there, lying flat against the grass bank and looking cautiously over the top. Where was the enemy? Not the faintest sign of him anywhere, nothing except the cows that had become restless and were gadding about. One, as I watched, rose on its hind legs, and then collapsed in a heap on the ground. And still the bullets kept coming, over our heads and all about us.[4] I searched through my glasses. Yes, there among the buildings away at the far end of the meadow was a faint haze of smoke. Then in God's name let us get closer.

3   A patrol of A Squadron 19th Hussars (5th Divisional Cavalry). The squadron had crossed the canal during the morning with orders to reconnoitre the line Tertre – Hautrage in front of the canal position of the 5th Division.

4   The sector of the canal position now being attacked by the Brandenburg Grenadiers was held as follows: It had been reached the previous evening (22nd) by the 13th Infantry Brigade; the 1st Royal West Kent Regiment occupied the canal crossings at St Ghislain, with a company in advance south of Tertre and supported by the 2nd Duke of Wellington's (West Riding) Regiment. On their left the 2nd King's Own Scottish Borderers and the machine-gun section 2nd King's Own Yorkshire Light Infantry held the line to and including the Les Herbières crossings, with the 2nd King's Own Yorkshire Light Infantry in support, the latter moving up and taking over the canal defence from the King's Own Scottish Borderers about 6 pm. The 1st East Surrey Regiment carried on the line along the canal bank west of Les Herbières.

"Forward again – at the double!" We crossed the track, jumped the broad dyke full of stagnant water on the far side, and then on across the squelching meadow. Tack, tack, tack, tack, tack! – srr – srr – huitt – tschiu – tschiu – tschirr! – cries – more lads falling.

"Down! Open fire – far end of meadow – range 1000 yards!"

And so we went on, gradually working forward by rushes of a hundred, later fifty, and then about thirty yards towards the invisible enemy. At every rush a few more fell, but one could do nothing for them. On, on, that was the only solution. Easier said than done, however, for not only was the meadow horribly swampy, filling our boots with water, but it was intersected by broad, water-logged drains and barbed-wire fences that had to be cut through.

Where was the rest of the battalion? Nothing to be seen of them Yes, there, a hundred yards to our left, a section of Grenadiers was working forward like us by short rushes, its leader, in front at every rush, taking giant strides. Why, it's the long-legged Fritz-Dietrich Gräser, he who sang the "*Krone am Rhein*" so well that evening at Weisweiler when we sat listening to the band with the old lady and her pretty niece. I'd known him for two years now, and a charming fellow he was. Now they were down again, this time along another broad water-drain with a barbed-wire fence along the enemy's side of it. And what was Gräser doing? Sure enough, he was running along the whole front of his section cutting the wire fence himself, in the middle of a burst of rifle and machine-gun fire. Plucky young devil?

Sergeant Holder-Egger now came up from behind with his two men, threw himself down in the muddy meadow beside me, panting for breath, and reported that he had handed the horses over to Lieutenant Grabert's section.

"There was another Englishman hidden in the farm," he said. "Lieutenant Grabert shot him with his revolver."

I looked again all round. The enemy was still invisible. Gräser was off again with his section, another long rush. He was now level with us, if anything slightly ahead.

"Lads!" I called out, "Do you see that? A Company is getting ahead of us. Can we allow it? Holder-Egger, on you go!"

"No. 1 Section – rush!" And so another thirty yards nearer the enemy, and about twelve in front of Gräser's section.

Gräser then, recognised me, and running up lay down beside me. "Sir," he said, gasping for breath, "I've got separated from my company. May I join you with my section?"

"Splendid! And welcome all of you to the Royal B Company. Another section – now I've quite an army again at my command!"

"It will be an honour, sir, for me to have my first fight under your orders."

He raised himself on his elbows, looked ahead, and then back at me, a flash of battle in his clear boyish eyes.

"Look, sir, do you see that white house over there? There's a machine gun in it. Shall we get it, sir?"

"Anyhow, I won't leave you in the lurch, Gräser; we'll try." I shouted down the line: "Advance by groups from the right, in short rushes." And then I heard Holder-Egger's voice as he led on forward.

From our new line I again searched the front through my glasses. Still no sign of the enemy. Only the unfortunate cows, now just ahead of us, and being between the two firing lines they were in a bad way, bellowing desperately, one after the other collapsing. To right and left, a cry here, a cry there: "I'm hit, sir! O God! Oh, mother! I'm done for!"

"I'm dying, sir!" said another near me. "I can't help you, my young man, we must go on – come, give me your hand."

Gräser's clear voice again: "On again – double!" On we went.

Behind us the whole meadow was dotted with little grey heaps. The hundred and sixty men that left the wood with me had shrunk to less than a hundred. But Grabert's section at my signal had now worked forward and prolonged our line to the right. He, too, had lost heavily, nevertheless there was still quite a respectable crowd of us gradually moving on, wave by wave, closer and closer to the invisible enemy. We officers had some time previously taken a rifle from a dead or wounded man, filled – our pockets with cartridges, and were firing away into the haze of smoke at the far end of the meadow. I felt, however, that these continuous rushes were telling on the men, and that they must have a breathing space.

"Stop for a bit!" I shouted down the line. "No further advance without my orders!"

I noticed that at this period of the advance if one lay quite flat, the enemy's fire always passed over one, that it was, in fact, slightly high all the time we were lying down. It appeared very strange at the time, and it was not until several months later when a wounded friend was showing me photographs he had taken afterwards of the English position, that I saw the reason. At the end of this meadow was a canal with an embankment on either side. The enemy's position was on the farther embankment, so that he had to fire over the embankment on our side, and as we were crossing a flat meadow below the canal level, this near-side embankment made a lot of dead ground for us, the shelter of which naturally became more pronounced the nearer we got to the canal. The machine-gun fire from the houses on this side of the canal seemed to have been silenced – they were hammering no more at us anyhow.

We were now about 500 yards from the canal bank. A few paces in front lay some of the miserable cows in horrible death agonies. While I was meditating on the situation I suddenly heard a voice on my left saying: "Gräser, would you like a glass of champagne?" I was dumbfounded. On my immediate left lay a private of A Company, unknown to me, then came Gräser, then a long, lanky corporal with a face marked both with a look of drink and with several long scars across his left cheek. Glancing at him I remembered his face, that of a student who had served his year with the colours in A Company some time back. I had heard that there was a doctor, a former student, who had joined up and had done his army service with that company, and so I now imagined this was the man. Anyhow it was from his lips had come the amazing offer to Gräser.

I shall never forget the look on the others' faces as this unknown corporal, taking his rifle in his right hand, put his left into his haversack and out of it produced, with a giggle of triumph, a golden-necked bottle.

"Well, I'll be damned, Knopfe!" said Gräser. "Where the devil did you find that?"

The old student laughed slyly: "It found itself in my haversack."

"Wonderful! Pass it along. Who knows, it may be our last drink!" And then, turning to me, Gräser asked: "Have you a cup by any chance, sir?"

"I have, but you'll only get it on the condition that I have a smack as well."

"But of course!" laughed Gräser. "The captain and I, and the lucky owner, Knopfe, and my gallant orderly here, Blöse, we four, in these pleasant surroundings, will empty the bottle to the health of the regiment."

I handed over my aluminium drinking-cup, the cork popped – and there, lying flat on our stomachs all the time, five hundred yards from the English position, we four finished the bottle of champagne between us. Yes, quite comfortably, with the enemy's bullets almost shaving the tops of our heads. Gräser shared out his last cigarettes and there we lay for a while smoking, stretched out flat.

"Well, gentlemen, now we've got the necessary courage inside we can go on!" and looking down the line I shouted: "Advance by short rushes from the right!" and the order was passed along.

From now on the English fire gradually weakened, almost ceased. No hail of bullets greeted each rush forward, and we were able to get within 150 yards of the canal bank. I said to Gräser: "Now we'll do one more 30-yard rush, all together, then fix bayonets and charge the houses and the canal banks."

The enemy must have been waiting for this moment to get us all together at close range, for immediately the line rose it was as if the hounds of hell had been loosed at us, yelling, barking, hammering as a mass of lead swept in among us.

"Down!" I shouted, and on my left I heard through the din Gräser's voice repeating it. Voluntarily and in many cases involuntarily, we all collapsed flat on the grass as if swept by a scythe.

Previously after each rush Gräser had brightened us up with a commentary of curses and cheery chatter, but now there was a noticeable silence on my left.

"Gräser!" I called out. No answer. "Where is Lieutenant Gräser?" And then from among the cries and groans all round came a low-voiced reply: "Lieu-tenant Gräser is dead, sir, just this moment. Shot through the head and heart as he fell. He's here."

I was speechless, as if someone had caught me by the throat, choking me. Gräser dead. – Incredible! A moment ago sparkling with life, fun, and the devil's own courage: now dead. Then it had indeed been his last drink!

From now on matters went from bad to worse. Wherever I looked, right or left, were dead or wounded, quivering in convulsions, groaning terribly, blood oozing from fresh wounds. The worst was that the heaviest firing now began to come on us from the strip of wood that jutted out into the meadow to our right rear: It must be our own men, I thought, who could not imagine we had got on so far and now evidently took us for the enemy. Luckily we had a way of stopping that: "Who has the red flag?" Grenadier Just produced it, and lying on his back waved it wildly. No result; in fact the fire from the right rear became even heavier. The brave Just stood up and with complete unconcern continued to wave the red flag more frantically than ever. But still no effect.

"Lie down, Just, good fellow, you've done well but it's no use; they must see but they won't believe."

I blew my whistle full blast and any of the NCO's with whistles did the same. Still no good. The firing continued, more and more of my men were being hit.[5] I

5   This fire was from the machine-gun section of the East Surrey Regiment and part of C Company that were in position in this strip of wood.

discovered too at this time that we had scarcely any ammunition left; and here we were, isolated and 120 yards from the English position. Next to me was a Grenadier hit through both cheeks and tongue, his face a mass of blood; and beyond him Pohlenz, my bugler, a bullet hole through the bugle slung on his back, the homemade cigarette in the corner of his mouth, and himself firing shot after shot, as calmly as an old philosopher, at the garden of the white house in front. He declared he'd seen someone moving in it.

"Pohlenz, my lad, stop firing. We must keep every round we've got in case those fellows across the canal make a counter-attack on us. Instead, you must make your way back as quick as you can to the battalion, find the major and tell him that B Company is here, has no more ammunition, and has had heavy losses and wants reinforcements and ammunition."

He repeated the message. "B Company is close up against the English position, heavy losses, no more cartridges, wants reinforcements and ammunition," then put another cigarette, rolled in the interval between his two last shots, in the left corner of his mouth, stood up in the most casual manner and went back. Bullets seemed to come at him from all directions, but he appeared to have a charmed life and went leisurely on.

Where were the others? Where was Holder-Egger? I called his name: "Wounded in the last rush – he's lying ten paces behind you, sir." I crawled back to him. There he lay, the fine young fellow, on his back, a hole in his coat and a trickle of blood marking a wound in the stomach. His eyes stared motionless up to the evening sky.

"How are you, Holder-Egger?"

He turned his head feebly towards me. "It's all over with me. I'm done, sir," he said lifelessly.

"Oh, nonsense. Is the wound dressed?"

"No, captain." He closed his eyes and seemed to shrink away into himself. I listened; he was still breathing. Opening the blood-soaked coat I found the wound and tried to bandage it, bringing the bandage-tapes round under him, but it was difficult and the bleeding didn't stop. I looked round for help, and a few paces from Gräser's corpse saw Corporal Knopfe's lanky figure, the dispenser of the champagne.

"Knopfe!" I called out, "come here, doctor, and help dress this man's wound."

He crawled back to me and made a first-rate job of it. Of course being a doctor he should, I thought. "Come along, doctor, and let's bandage up some of the other poor devils." And off we started, getting grateful glances mixed with groans of agony for our reward.

"Please, sir, I've such a thirst!"

"I'm sorry, lad, but I've left my flask on my horse."

"I've some, sir," said Knopfe, and he gave the parched throat refreshment.

"Will you bandage me too, sir," came a voice from the right, "I'm in such pain!"

"Yes, my little lad, we're just coming," and so it went on.

The fire began again from the front – srr – srr – tschiu – tschuitt! all among us. One of the wounded men was hit a second time, another unwounded got hit through the head and just relaxed dead.

"Soon, at this rate, not one of us will be left alive," muttered Knopfe sullenly. From the white house a machine gun traversed once, twice, three times all the length of our line, followed by a message passed down from the right: "Lieutenant Grabert very badly wounded, sir." Good God, he too! The burden of responsibility was becoming appalling, insupportable.

"Come along, doctor, we must go and dress Grabert's wound. But keep very close to the ground so that in front they'll think we're all dead. A few more like the last and we all shall be."

We wriggled along like a couple of snakes behind the row of hob-nailed boots of the living and the dead.

"Why do you keep calling me doctor?" asked Knopfe as we went. "My subject is philology, not medicine. You must be mixing me with Warnecke, who is with C Company."

"Yes, I did think you were a doctor. Where did you learn to dress a wound so well?"

"In the same place as you learnt it, sir."

Students from the same university – a smile, a laugh was irresistible even here in the middle of this grizzly battlefield, as a mass of joyous scenes of the university life of our youth flashed unspoken through our minds … "Vaterland, du land des Ruhmes weih zu deines Heiligtumes Hütern, Hütern uns und unser Schwert …"

There lay poor Grabert, a deathly pallor over his strong face. "Where are you hit, Grabert?" He pointed to his waist. I opened the blood-stained coat but found the skin unmarked. "No, it isn't there," I said, and he then pointed to his right shoulder. This was more probable, as the chest and right sleeve of his coat were soaked through with blood. I got out my war-knife, that wonderful knife with so many odds and ends in it that I had bought the day before mobilisation, that day of shopping with you, dear wife, in Stuttgart. For a second as I took it out a flood of memories came to me from far, ever so far away, from another, a lost world, lost maybe for ever. It was a long and difficult job. He had had at least three machine-gun bullets through him. His right shoulder was shot clean through, and two bullets through the right breast which must have pierced his lung. We dressed his wounds as best we could, getting some more bandages from the dead alongside.

All this time the rifle-fire was continuing from the canal bank, but so long as we kept flat and our heads well down the bullets passed just over us. The sky was beginning to redden in the west; if only night would come quickly. I looked back for any sign of reinforcements or ammunition being sent up. Nothing coming, nothing. Yes, one man. It was Pohlenz. Brave lad, I'd given him up some time since as dead. But there he was, fired at from all directions, and he cared not; still a cigarette between the narrow lips of his happy-go-lucky, gutter-snipe face. He lay down beside me and took out of his pockets four packets of cartridges: "The major says we are to stay where we are, and the battalion will soon be coming up to us bringing ammunition with them. And here's a little to carry on with." He opened the packets and threw the chargerfuls to left and right, eager hands reaching out for them. "And here's a regimental order."

I unrolled the scrap of paper from a field note-book. "According to orders from Brigade Headquarters a general attack will be made on the bridges at 6.30 pm" On the bridges! Of course, the canal bridges. The map showed a thing like a bridge near the group of houses half-right called Les Herbières. Good! when the others come up we'll go on with them. To go on alone now would be idiotic. I looked at my watch. The attack was to be at 6.30. It was already 7 pm.

"What's happening back there?" I asked Pohlenz.

"The battalion is three or four hundred yards behind us."

"Many losses?"

Pohlenz beat the air with his hands two or three times. "Grey corpses lying all over the meadow."

"Have all the companies had losses?"

"All of them, sir."

Damn! The enemy were firing like madmen again. Astounding that any of us still lived. The bullets hummed about me like a swarm of angry hornets. I felt death, my own death, very, very near me; and yet it was all so strangely unreal. How many times had I not experienced all this in my imagination during the writing of those war-novels, and yet now, just this one time, I was asked to believe it to be solid fact. Nevertheless death did not come to me, so very close but not yet; and while I lived I would at least help all I could. "Come along, Knopfe; someone just behind wants us."

It must have been some hours, it seemed an eternity, before gradually the dusk came, terribly slowly, but at last it began to cover us. The assault on the bridges must have been put off, for the battalion did not appear. Another of my splendid lads was bandaged up, and then I wiped the blood off my knife and hands and rested a moment. Near me lay Corporal Grandeit, one of the bravest and most cheerful of men, smoking a cigarette. He evidently noticed a look of longing in my glance.

"Will you have one, sir?"

"My good friend, you have no idea … no, it's your last. You must keep it."

"Please, sir, I insist. You must take it," and his fingers, covered with blood and mud, placed the little roll of bliss in my mouth; and, God! how wonderful it tasted, the best in a lifetime! And, spite of all, how very good it was, lying here with all these splendid, loyal hearts beating around me, some cold, but the rest steadily, strongly beating, and all of them valiant. I began to experience that amazing bond of friendship that springs up between those who are facing death, risking all, together. Children, almost I love you.

In the half-light there was suddenly a stir behind us. Reinforcements; actually reinforcements. It was von der Osten and his group. He had followed the embankment to the wood, and after that had not been able to find us again. He had asked everywhere for B Company but none knew where it had gone. Finally by following up the trail of dead and wounded, recognising them by the company tassel on the bayonet-scabbard, he had arrived, each of his nine men, with two hundred and fifty rounds apiece. This ammunition was quickly distributed along the line and another effort made to silence the machine gun in the upper room of the white house.

"Two rounds each at the white house. Aim just below the eaves of the roof!" Through my glasses I could see in the failing light that at least no window pane was left. The gun was silent for a while, maybe altogether, I never knew. As the darkness deepened the din of battle all along the line quietened down, and then quite distinctly from behind came a bugle-call, the 1st Battalion "assembly." Surely we had not to go back, to give up what we had gained? But the call was repeated again and again. We had to obey; it was impossible for us to judge the general situation, and, no doubt, it was for the best. It was now too dark for the enemy to see. I got up on my legs, my limbs all stiff and hurting as if they'd been drawn from their sockets. The dampness of the meadow and the soaking in the dykes had wetted my clothes through to the skin. Nevertheless I was up, actually standing up.

"Did you hear that, lads? We have to go back. But we must take the wounded with us." The pieces of tent-cloth carried by each man were tied to rifles and on these extemporised stretchers all the wounded were gradually collected. It meant hard work for the others and took time, but it had to be done in spite of protests from some of the wounded themselves, though others were only too willing to be moved, and in any case they couldn't be left where they were.

"Me too, sir, me too!" "Of course, lad, only be patient, and wait your turn.2

Knopfe did not leave my side, and Pohlenz, Niestrawski, Sauermann all joined us. Marvellous, my three trusty staff, not a hair of any of them touched. Thanks to the darkness all went well. No more bullets came from the canal bank, only in the distance an occasional crackle of musketry. So conscientious were we in those early days of the war that we collected all the rifles we could find and many of the packs to take back with us. I had five rifles slung over my shoulder as we slowly processed stage by stage back with our groaning burdens to the battalion, back across the same waterlogged dykes we had jumped a few hours before. Now and again one's foot hit against something soft – a corpse. Our bones were so weary we could hardly carry on, but it had to be done. Some of the dykes were so broad that armfuls of sticks and faggots had to be fetched from the wood and thrown in to make a way across. At times, hearing the movement of the procession, a voice would call through the darkness: "Friends, help me. Come and take me back." "We're coming; we'll take you with us." And any who had no burden went out in search of the despairing cry to bring him in.

All at once I heard a familiar voice in front: Spiegel's, surely – Spiegel, commanding A Company. A flood of curses and then a sobbing, a whimpering like a sick girl. The old East African veteran. "Here, someone, take these a moment!" In the darkness a black figure came near, took the great weight off my shoulders on to his own and in a moment I was kneeling by Spiegel's side. I struck a match and looked with horror into the face of a fast dying man. An NCO beside him said to me: "Several of us wished to stay with him and get him back, but he raged at us and told us to get away, that we were wanted more in front." As it was, nothing more could be done, except an injection of morphia to give him a painless death. Perhaps that was possible if we took him back with us. In a few moments another stretcher made with rifles and canvas was ready, and strong hands lifted on to it, with a wonderful tenderness, the heavy body heaving from side to side in its agonies. "Goodnight, Spiegel," and in my thoughts I knew as well as he did we should see each other by daylight no more.

Exhausted, I lay down for a few moments' rest, and then up again after the dark forms of my tireless, marvellous men plodding on ahead. And now other dark forms were coming towards us. Stretcher-bearers – the regimental band doing a less cheerful job. "I hope you will find very little to do in front there. We've got the wounded with us here, but go and look all the same in case."

Through the darkness came the clink of spades, and low voices.

"Who's there?"

"A Company."

"What are you doing?"

"Digging in. Battalion orders."

"Is the major anywhere about?"

"He was here a moment ago, and went off to the left."

I went after him, groping my way along behind the line of black, ghostly shapes working with their spades, and found him.

"Two sections of B and one of A Company have rejoined the battalion, sir."

Major von Kleist, a head taller than me, stood facing me in the darkness, so dark that I couldn't see his features, and laying his two hands on my shoulders said in a heart-broken voice: "My dear Bloem, you are now my only support."

"How do you mean, major? You surely don't say – "

"Yes, Count Reventlow is seriously wounded, a bullet through the shoulder. He remained with his company for some hours after it, but I've ordered him to go back. Spiegel is said to have been wounded beyond hope of recovery – "

"I know, major. I've just seen him and had him brought in."

"And Goerdt, commanding D Company, is dead."

I was dumbfounded. "And the other officers? and the men?"

"It's unspeakable, terrible. I've just heard too that Major Prager, one of the first to enter Tertre, has been killed." Prager, the gallant commander of the Fusilier battalion, an East African veteran like Spiegel, with all his bad and excellent qualities.

"Von Hagen, the adjutant of the regiment, has been wounded; while of our first battalion, Gräser is said to be dead, Sehmsdorf of A Company wounded, and little Grapow of the machine-gun company dead. I don't yet know how the other battalions have fared, but it seems to have been terrible for them all. What a day, Bloem, perfectly ghastly!"

"And the men?"

"The battalion is all to pieces – my splendid battalion," and the voice of this kindly, big-hearted man trembled as he spoke. "I've given orders to entrench 200 yards in front of the road leading to the wood. Will you see to that while the rest of the companies get reorganised? You will have to give up von der Osten, who will take command of A Company. Chorus will take over C Company, and Löhmann, D Company."

Three subalterns as company commanders, two of them officers of the reserve, and my own subalterns all gone. I listened in silence, anxiously, as the major continued. "Watch the front very carefully, and send patrols at once up to the line of the canal. If the English have the slightest suspicion of the condition we are in they will counter-attack tonight, and that would be the last straw. They would send us all to glory. Have bayonets fixed ready, and every section digging or resting must have a sentry on watch. Will you go and see to that now? I am relying on you."

"Right, major."

How inky dark was this night; not a glimmer of light. So that was our first battle, and this was the result. Our grand regiment, with all its pride and splendid discipline, its attack full of dash and courage, and now only a few fragments left. In God's name, what was the meaning of it all?

I groped my way back behind the line of black, ghostly figures still shovelling away, but the trench was a failure. Two spade-depths down into the meadow and the water-level was reached; after that the water oozed up at once and filled it. I searched for the new company commanders and gave them the major's instructions, and together we tried to get the companies formed up again.

My other section also turned up with Sergeant Schüler. He and half his section had been kept back as a covering party for the artillery and had had very few casualties, but of the rest of the section with Tettenborn only a few remained alive, their leader having been shot while looking through his field-glasses. Farewell, friend, you will not be forgotten.

I began to shiver from head to foot, chilled to the very marrow in my sopping clothes and with the damp night mist. From one of the packs brought back I unstrapped a waterproof cape and put it round me. No sooner done than I heard another familiar voice through the darkness:

"Captain Bloem! Anyone seen Captain Bloem?"

"Ahlert!" Good for him; and somehow I felt he had brought something with him, something to comfort us. In a moment a dark figure stood in front of me, but indistinguishable in this blackest of nights.

"Here, sir."

"Ahlert, my good Ahlert, have you heard what's happened?"

"I know, sir. It's terrible."

"Thank Heaven, you're all right anyhow," I said, taking his strong, honest hand in mine. "Did you get much of the fire back there?"

"Not so bad, sir."

"How are the horses, the cooker, the transport?"

"All safe, sir. We took good care of them, and we're bringing up coffee now for the company." I heard a clattering of tin mugs.

"Thanks be to God, coffee, hot coffee! B Company," I called out, "one man from each section this way."

Miraculous! Coffee, here on the battlefield. Only lukewarm, naturally, still it was coffee. Ahlert, bless you!

And now for the outposts. Ahlert helped me get the patrols together. It was no easy matter in this pitch darkness, in the indescribable confusion, and the men all chilled to the bone, almost too exhausted to move and with the depressing consciousness of defeat weighing upon them. A bad defeat, there could be no gainsaying it; in our first battle we had been badly beaten, and by the English – by the English we had so laughed at a few hours before.

I gave the patrols their orders, sending the best NCO's I had left with them – Wolff, Boettcher and Kraullss. "If the English make an attack give the alarm by a volley, and then move away at once to the right so that we shall have a clear field of fire." I felt a lump in my throat as these gallant men went off and disappeared into the night, in the direction of the enemy. I should have liked to accompany each of the patrols myself; instead I had to be content to watch them go, a little lesson in self-control one quickly has to learn in war-time.

I went back to the others, to the line of black, ghostly shapes still digging. "Now, men, we must chuck this. It's no use. We can't lie in a trench full of water. Each of you must find as dry a spot as you can near by and go to sleep."

I was about to lie down myself when I again heard my name being called. It was Erdmann Gräser, the elder brother of the dead one, and the adjutant of the Fusilier battalion. There he stood facing me, only recognisable by his voice.

"Have you heard already, Gräser?"

"I have, sir." His voice sounded hard and dry.

"Your brother, Gräser; that fine, plucky brother of yours."

"Can I – see him once more, sir?"

"But how can you? We have retired five or six hundred yards, and he lies away at the farthest point we reached, only about a hundred yards from the English position. Besides you'd never find him, and very likely you'd run into the enemy's hands on the way. But I can tell you how he died, and I can imagine no finer death for a soldier."

And I told the brother the story of his brother's death. I could not see his face as I related it, but no sound, no interruption came from his lips, not a murmur till I had finished.

"I'm most grateful to you, sir."

"Good-night, Gräser."

"Good-night, sir." A short but firm clasp of my hand and he was away again into the night. I stretched myself out again on the dripping wet grass. A few stars were twinkling up above through the low night-mist overhanging the meadow. And they made me think of my own far-away constellations – my wife, my children. If they could see me now; no, it's as well they can't. Goodnight, my precious ones. In spirit I am with you, close to you.

I could not sleep. Though all my strength seemed to have left me and I was dog-tired, yet sleep would not come. I dozed lightly. Would they attack to-night?[6] Let them, and they'll find it expensive. Disorganised little rabble though we now were, we should only sell our lives at a big price.

Suddenly a tremendous burst, like an explosion, not far away either; a terrifying noise. A few moments later another. Everyone jumped to their feet. What on earth was it? Certainly not a gun of any kind. A rumour ran round that it was the bridges, that the English had blown up the canal bridges.[7] Surely impossible! The English blow up bridges! Nonsense, it must have been something else; but what? In trying to answer the question for myself I must have dozed off again, for when another loud report woke me, the first light of dawn had arrived. This time it was the artillery, our own artillery near Tertre station close by, and they now began to fire continuously, the whirring noise of the shells fading away as they sped across the canal southwards, followed by the faint, dull bursts in the distance. All this fire from our own guns gave us confidence; it was good to listen to.

6   The British retirement from the St Ghislain – Les Herbières line began soon after 10pm, though not completed till after 2am.

7   The bridges at St Ghislain were blown up by the 17th Field Company RE at 1.30 am (24th). Those at Les Herbières had been blown up previously about 8 pm

Around me my grey men were still snoring away. The dawn light shed a deathly pallor over their faces, but their lips moved slightly with each breath. I shuddered with wet and cold, nevertheless I felt refreshed, a revival of energy. And I was alive. What joy incredible! still alive. I wondered did my loved ones feel that I still lived. I stretched, my clothes all sticking to me, and then once more dropped off again, and when I woke the new day was already glimmering in the east.

Chapter Eleven

The Advance Is Resumed

The battalion adjutant, Lieutenant Stumpff, was standing by me. I got up. In spite of his rosy face I could see how much he had felt the death of little Grapow, his great friend and brother-in-law.

"My deepest sympathy, Stumpff."

"Thank you, sir." And then he continued in more official tones: "Battalion orders are as follows: The enemy has evacuated all his positions on this side of the canal during the night and blown up the bridges behind him. The Fusilier battalion is already deploying and will advance on the canal. The 1st Battalion will assemble in column of route and march to the bridges at St Ghislain: companies in the following order, B, A, C, D."

I listened speechless with amazement. Positions evacuated! Bridges blown up! Advance on the canal! Incredible. And so the explosions during the night were explained.

"Do I understand you rightly, Stumpff? Has the enemy actually retired?"

"No doubt about it, sir."

"Well, I'm damned! Then things aren't so bad after all."

"It's too early to judge the situation for certain," he said. "Perhaps it's only a ruse to entice us over the canal."

"In any case, we're going on forwards, Stumpff! That's good enough."

In a few moments all were on their legs and bustling about. Ahlert was again on the spot with pailfuls of more lukewarm coffee. How good it was too! Waterproofs rolled, coats buttoned, belts tightened up, and in five minutes the battalion was ready to move off. Our artillery fire had stopped, no sound of battle anywhere, peace, perfect peace once more – and we were advancing. Marvellous! The companies, yesterday at full war strength, were now scarcely at peace strength, yet they were going – forwards! And the sun, the giver of health and life, yesterday clouded over, was now rising higher and higher into a cloudless sky.

Along the borders of the village engineers were digging, digging hard, digging fresh graves, apparently countless fresh graves. Looking across we could see that our own dead had already disappeared into the cold swampy soil of the enemy's country. There were English dead too, gathered together here and there in small heaps in the village streets.[1] They were evidently to take second place in the burial programme. In a sense we were glad to see them, as it increased our self-confidence. Quite enough had happened to depress us.

The 2nd Battalion had assembled on the main road, and as we marched past them we greeted our still living friends, hearing news from them of more and more

---

1 Men of the 5th Divisional Cyclist Company, and of A Company 1st Royal West Kent Regiment, who lost two officers and fifty-eight other ranks before retiring from their advanced positions south of Tertre.

casualties. Otherwise the march was silent. The patrols sent out the evening before joined in the column as we approached the canal. Sergeant Boettcher, in making his report to me, said that the firing that had enfiladed us all the afternoon from the strip of wood on the right, and which we took to be our own people firing at us by mistake, had been the enemy all the time. He had been through the copse and had found a sandbag emplacement for a machine gun in it.[2] The dirty dogs! All the same we should have suspected it and taken better precautions during the advance.

Then they apparently did know something about war, these cursed English, a fact soon confirmed on all sides. Wonderful, as we marched on, how they had converted every house, every wall into a little fortress: the experience no doubt of old soldiers gained in a dozen colonial wars; possibly even some of the butchers of the Boers were among them. And now they'd gone, left all this work, rather than wait for our bayonets and the butts of our rifles.

The effect of our artillery had been shattering. Houses shelled to ruins everywhere. We saw for the first time war in all its frightfulness, its destruction, and devastation. Our field-howitzers had torn holes as big as windows through houses and factory walls; the roofs had been torn off as though by a hurricane. Well done, the guns!

Now we were at the famous canal. The bits of the blown-up bridges were lying about all round, but our engineers were already at work putting a pontoon bridge across for the artillery. Close by, a narrow iron foot-bridge had been left that could be swung across the brackish water of the canal. This we now had to cross in single file – and a long time it took. As each section got across, it piled arms the far side and rested. We heard that the 3rd Battalion of our sister-regiment, the 52nd, had already crossed with two companies of our Fusilier battalion. Our 2nd Battalion was to cross the canal about 1000 yards farther east.

In a seemingly interminable procession, man by man, the companies continued to cross, assembling opposite the railway station of St Ghislain, which lay on our right in profound sleep and badly knocked about. Another order now arrived from regimental headquarters: "The enemy has taken up a fresh position on the rising ground south of Hornu. The brigade is to attack. Battalions will take up preparatory positions as follows: 3rd Battalion 52nd Regiment with its right on the main street, 1st Battalion 12th Grenadiers on its immediate left, 2nd and Fusilier Battalion 12th Grenadiers to follow in echelon."

From now on as each company crossed the bridge it was to go to its position for the advance on Hornu. The deployment for the attack was to take place from the southern exits of the village as soon as the assembly was complete.

Good! B Company was ready. "Stand-to." The men unpiled arms and then we were off again. "March at ease." The morning sun blazed down upon the deserted streets and squares of this little industrial town. It looked strange to see all the houses and shops barred and shuttered, and stranger still the traces of our bombardment, the smashed-in roofs covering the streets with broken tiles and chimney-pots. At a street corner, in front of a grocer's shop, the door of which had been smashed open with an axe, stood General Sontag, our brigade commander. Busy hands kept passing out to him from inside masses of packets of chocolates, biscuits,

2   See footnote, p. 43

and cakes, which he distributed to the troops as they passed. A hundred greedy hands stretched out to him, and greedy eyes from a hundred hungry faces tried to catch his.

But listen! Over there to the south the noise of battle was beginning again. Rifle-fire already, and our deployment hardly begun; it would be hours before we were ready to attack, thanks to that confounded footbridge. Even as we listened the firing increased in intensity. Surely the 52nd hadn't started without waiting for us.

It would be utter madness. The noise of battle drew us forward magnetically and we hurried on, the sweat pouring off us.

Once away from the houses we were able to get a view to the south, and saw a number of giant black pyramids standing out against the sky. Being a son of the industrial west I knew what they were, these conical hills; they were slag-heaps of mine refuse. We had passed from the agricultural northern district of the Hennegau into the mining district, and the town of St Ghislain, as also the village of Hornu which is practically the continuation of it southwards, bore the stamp of their trade, even though the inhabitants had departed. A mass of rough brick-buildings, all dirty, all joyless, and all most unlovable.

A shot suddenly, right into the column, from quite close. Damn it! another, and another. They were coming not from the houses close to the road but from some higher buildings behind. Perhaps civilians, perhaps English stragglers, perhaps both! Yet another, the dirty dogs! Right in the middle of the company, and more still; here and there suddenly the clatter of a rifle on the cobbles and a grenadier, clutching the air with his hands, collapsed in a heap on the road. But there was no time to search the building or even to set fire to it, for at that moment Lieutenant Maron, now adjutant of the regiment in place of Hagen, wounded yesterday, galloped towards us from the front, the sparks literally flying from the cobbled stones beneath his horse's hoofs as he came. In a shrill voice and out of breath he shouted: "The 52nd heavily engaged in front – need support immediately – please hurry on!" and then he spurred his horse on again to tell the others behind.

Almost at the same moment the air just above our heads was rent by a howling scream that rushed straight down the narrow street between the houses and then burst with a great crack, like the splitting of big timber, just behind the last section of fours, scattering a hail of shot into the cobbles, sending up more sparks and a cloud of dust and chips of stone. Shrapnel! the first we had met. And looking at my men I saw many a face turn pale that yesterday had smiled defiantly as the machine-gun fire traversed to and fro along the line. Another tearing scream, and another, four in close succession – gorr! – gorr! – gorr! – gorr! and four bursts – crash! – crash! – crash! – crash! above our heads, but this time on to the roofs of the houses, and a rain of broken slates rattled down on to our helmets and shoulders. A most devilish, damnable feeling! In a moment the company had moved to the left side of the road, close under the houses to get what cover they could, the shells coming if anything from that direction. It delayed the march at a moment when we were needing wings to get us forward fast enough.

"Come on, lads, didn't you hear? Our friends in front are in danger. Now then, we'll run for it, and whoever hangs back and leaves his captain is a damned coward! Double!" The word of command pulled the flagging ones together, the iron discipline that had been drilled into them conquered. Their rifles over their right shoulder and holding their bayonets with their left hand in drill-book manner my men trotted along behind me, while more shrapnel screamed above us, to right and to left of us, bursting and scattering their loads of bullets with a noise like the hounds of hell vomiting. Trapp – trapp – trapp – trapp! the steady foot-falls of the hob-nailed boots of my men resounded along the empty street in the intervals of the din, the rifle and artillery fire increasing continually as we approached the battle, shrapnel bullets, rifle bullets, showers of broken tiles, chimney-pots, bits of stones, bricks, clouds of dust, the howling and screaming of the shells, and yet trapp – trapp – trapp – trapp! we kept on through it all.

At the crossing of a side street with the main street we were following stood some of the brigade and regimental staff. General Sontag, here already, watched us keenly, with Colonel von Reuter, amazingly calm and utterly unperturbed as a shower of broken tiles snowed down from the roofs above. Still doubling at the head of my company I saluted with a feeling of intense pride. "Down there to the left!" the general called out, pointing with his hand. "Prolong the left of the 52nd!"

"I understand, general!" And in a few long strides I was at the head of my men again and leading them down the narrow side-street. Here, we were covered from fire from the south by the houses, workmen's dwellings, miserable, dirty-looking hovels, and all shuttered up. Occasionally shot rattled on the roofs, but most of the shells passed over the top of us and away to the left.

Now the street came to an end, in place of the houses a long factory wall bordered the right-hand side, rifle and machine-gun bullets buzzing and humming over it in a countless stream, interspersed at short intervals with shrapnel bursts. Ahead, at a half-open iron gate at the wall end, stood Lieutenant Löhmann with a dozen men of D Company, of which he was now company commander.

"What's happening, Löhmann?"

"We can't get on any farther yet, sir. The fire's hellish; no one could live in it in the open." He seemed to be right. I looked back and saw two small groups of sweating, dusty, panting Grenadiers behind me.

"What's this? Where's the rest of the company?"

"Don't know, sir," answered an NCO (I had no officers now left with the company.) I was furiously disappointed. Four-fifths of the company to have left their commander in the lurch! And my own company! Surely, not possible! Luckily one of my cyclists was there, and I sent him back to fetch the rest. At the moment there was nothing more to be done except to carry out the order to prolong the left of the 52nd with the few men I had. But, where was the 52nd? I peeped round the gate-post, and drew back again very quickly as a bullet whistled past my nose. Damn it! Had we to go on through that? "You're quite right, Löhmann, it's distinctly windy out there."

Nevertheless we had to find out where we were to go, or at any rate where the 52nd was. To the right the ground was flat and open at first, then rose gradually up to a ridge beyond which was obviously the English position. From where we stood we could see the backs of the houses along the main village street we had just left, which rose on to the ridge in its southward course. This row of houses, with strips of cabbage-patches behind, stopped before the road topped the ridge, and there, just beyond and on the ridge itself, lay sure enough a firing-line of grey figures; that must be them, our hard-pressed sister regiment. Hard-pressed they were too, for small clouds of coal-black dust were continually spurting up along the line – bursting shrapnel. We had to get to them, somehow.

To prolong the left of the line, however, our way was blocked by an enormous conical slag-heap, the base of it reaching close up to the factory gate. If only we could get to the top of it, I thought, what a perfect field of fire we should have. The English had obviously done this, for most of their machine-gun and rifle-fire was coming from the upper slopes of two more giant slag-heaps, the tops of which appeared well above the skyline of the ridge.[3] Let us try them!

Soon we two officers and the two dozen men, all we now had, were starting to clamber up the steep slope of rubble. We dug our toes and hands into the crunching, crumbling coal-black slag, but it was no good. At every step up it gave beneath one's feet and slid down; the whole surface of the pyramid seemed the same, and so we abandoned the idea, streaming with sweat again and breathless with the effort.

The cyclist had now returned, and reported that the general had called the company back, just after we turned off from the main street, and told them to go straight on to the end of the village: the order, however, had not reached the head of the company, nor me, and so the remainder had stopped, gone back, and continued up the main street, Sergeant Schüler taking command of them. In God's name, then, let us make straight across to the main street again and find the others. I decided to rush for it, through the factory yard and then across a bit of open ground to the backs of the houses at the village end. Shrapnel bullets, rifle bullets hummed and whistled all round and about us, the noise enough to drive one crazy, now one man tumbling over, then another, and another. At last, clambering over a rotten wooden fence and crossing a miserable cabbage-patch of a garden, and along a path between the houses we were in the main street again. Here a few groups of Grenadiers were working forward by short rushes from house to house in brief intervals in the firing. But the enemy naturally guessed that it would be from here, from the village end, that the reinforcements would move up to support the front line on the ridge, and he kept it well smothered in showers of lead, almost without a break.

Most strange it was to see these houses, so recently inhabited, shot asunder, knocked to pieces. It was as if they themselves had suddenly gone mad and begun to spit out stones, dirt, bits of iron bedsteads, roofing slates, deliberately over us and over the memory of their late inhabitants. The whole atmosphere was impregnated with a rusty-coloured smoke, with brick dust that stuck in one's lungs, and filled one's eyes, heavy and burning after an almost sleepless night.

At last a breathing space, a moment to look round. To the left of the street we could now see quite distinctly the firing-line of the 52nd which we were to prolong. It was slightly bent back, its right flank towards the enemy, and into it the shrapnel were still pouring their mass of bullets. Smoke, dirt, and rubble were spurting up all along it. Could it be possible that any single man in that line still lived? A few brave ones now rushed out from the cover of the end houses to support the line – gorr! –

3   The line here, immediately east of the Wasmes-Hornu road, was held by the 2nd Duke of Wellington's (West Riding) Regiment. The battalion lost over 300 all ranks in this day's fighting. West of the road were two companies of the Dorset Regiment, with the 2nd King's Own Yorkshire Light Infantry in a position on the slag-heaps in rear of the front line.

gorr! – gorr! screamed the shells – crash! – crash! – crash! as they burst in the middle of them, and not a single one of the little group was left standing.

Simple madness, then, to try and get forward like that. Was there no other way of approach? I looked at my map. Yes, a railway appeared to run through a cutting near by. If we could get into that? What do you think, Löhmann? Yes – agreed. Good. "Now, men, all out, hard as you can, follow me – rush!" We raced over a stretch of open ground, threw ourselves down during the bursts of fire, then up and on again, reached the edge of the cutting, slid and jumped down its steep side, and then stood on the track, for a moment wonderfully protected from fire but also from seeing anything. The next thing was to climb up the other side and see what could be done. It was very steep. I clambered up a little way, then on all fours, using my sword-scabbard as a stick to push myself up, but I couldn't reach the top: exhausted I slid back on to the track. As it happened I had no need to be ashamed of myself for none of my Grenadiers, though twenty years younger, were able to do it. I noticed there seemed to be very few of them with me, only four of my own company, about a dozen from the rest of the battalion, and a few 52nd men. Lieutenant Löhmann had vanished, and, instead, Lieutenant Count Westarp had joined our little group, the left sleeve of his coat slit up by a bullet, his wrist slightly grazed and bound up with a blood-stained handkerchief.

We were all now back on the rails again, panting and dripping with perspiration, not a breath left in our lungs. "Well, lads, that's no good." I saw they were all as done up as myself, and I decided to have a breather before going on.

"Rossberg, you still look full of life, see if you can get up the slope, and let us know what's beyond."

The lad made much ado, but he got there, and then called down: "The 52nd are on the ridge just in front, firing like mad straight ahead."

"Where are the enemy?"

"Can't see anything of them, sir."

"Thanks, Rossberg. Then call out to the nearest 52nd man that there are 2 officers and 18 men here at their disposal ready to support them when they want us or if the enemy attacks."

After a while came the reply: "They say, all right, sir."

Then we all lay down full length in the grass-covered ditch by the side of the track. Thank God, some rest! an oasis in the storm of the battle! A few moments under cover, a few moments in cooling shade! What bliss! And yet at the same time I felt it was clearly wrong to allow oneself this respite fifty yards behind the firing-line where every rifle, every man, must be urgently needed. But for the moment I – simply – couldn't – go – on. A comfortable feeling of helplessness overcame me, I was prostrate, my limbs declined to function. I called myself every name imaginable – sluggard, useless rotter, coward – but it made no difference, the machine wouldn't work, wouldn't even start. And my Grenadiers looked equally satisfied, equally content to stay where they were. Within five minutes many of them were snoring, mouths wide open, and above us across the top of the cutting, the hurricane of lead and iron still raged with unabated fury. Shells, whining, howling, rushed past above us, bullets whistled, hummed, and bumbled up and down the scale of the whole range of insect noises from the soft whirring of a dragon-fly to the loud buzzing of an angry cockchafer. They beat against the steel telegraph posts with a clear, sharp "pink," leaving a small, circular black spot on the grey painting, they cut the wires one after the other all hanging hopelessly entangled from the posts. And yet, just underneath, there we lay cosy and snug on the soft grass, so cool, so safe, so peaceful. How nice, how pleasant it was! Let the others shoot and fight if they want to – I simply can't. No! you lazy, worthless bit of carrion, you – simply – can't!

"Sir! the enemy are going back, sir!"

"What! what's that! The enemy going back? Coming forwards, you mean – "

"No, sir! The enemy are going back, the 52nd say so!" Rossberg shouted down from the top of the cutting.

"Get up, everyone! Quick, come on!" We scrambled up somehow, sideways, anyways, to the top, all idea of exhaustion blown away as if by magic. Behind me came the snorers of a moment before now keen as a troop of devils. Was it possible we had arrived too late for the victory after having slept through the battle? What a thought! We ran on up the gentle incline, took forward with us the weak supports of the 52nd, lying flat on their stomachs in a slight fold of the ground waiting the order to advance, and then came to the ridge along which the firing line had been. From here we could see a line of khaki-brown figures disappearing hastily among the slag-heaps, sheds, and trees ahead of us.

"Come on, lads, hurry up! Keep them on the run!" and taking every one on with us as we went, we doubled on in a jumbled mass, battalions, companies all mixed up together. Count Westarp and I were now joined by Lieutenant Wildegans, another of the regiment, a splendid fellow, always cheerful, thoroughly efficient, a typical 12th Grenadier.

"Get along, lads, no stopping, or they'll turn round and start firing again." We crossed the ridge and the bit of flat ground beyond, and came to the enemy's position, jumping the English trenches in which some of the dead were crouching life-like, their pale cheeks still on the butts of their rifles as if firing.[4] On! on! No time to wait! And then suddenly a terrible thing happened.

From behind us, from where we had come, a screaming, tearing noise, followed by a piercing crash, then another, a third, a fourth, and the last right in the middle of the densely packed group of men about me all hurrying on without thought of keeping extended out.

Since that day I have seen enough gruesome sights to make any man's blood curdle, but even now I still shudder at the thought of that moment. The great shout of terror from everyone, the yells of pain from two dozen throats around me, the look of open-eyed horror on every face, all mingled with the continued tearing, screaming, and bursting of the shells, and last but not least, my own heart almost standing still in agonised despair; never shall I forget that moment.

What had happened? In a flash it was only too clear. Our guns, which after the restoration of the bridges would by now be across the canal, must have at once opened fire on the enemy's position, which though invisible to them would have been very exactly described. These, then, were their first shots on to the English line, excellent shots too, only it so happened that our infantry by their own efforts had meanwhile stormed the position, a fact also beyond the sight and ken of the ar-

4   Most probably men of the 2nd Duke of Wellington's (West Riding) Regiment.

tillery observers in the low ground. Something had to be done at once, quick! The first was to understand the situation, the second to act, to save what was left to be saved, to clear out, not backwards nor forwards – both useless – then sideways it must be; anyhow, to clear out. "All follow me!" I yelled madly; Westarp and Wildegans repeated: "Follow the captain!" And sideways we fled, looking desperately for any scrap of cover. There! a slight hollow, not much, but just enough perhaps to shelter us from our own shells. "Down!" and all collapsed, many burying their pale, terrified faces in the short grass, hiding their heads in their folded arms as if instinctively to protect themselves. Death coming from the enemy's shells is expected, part of the bargain of war, but coming from the mistaken fire of one's own artillery it is beyond the pale – utterly devilish!

Only just in time. Twenty yards to our left the little white whiffs of smoke of the shrapnel burst every ten seconds; a little farther and we would be done for, even yet, but no! they gradually moved away to the left again. The enemy's artillery now opened again a rapid fire, shell after shell in quick succession, high over our stretched-out bodies, away over the ridge on which our firing-line had been and beyond, evidently in an effort to silence our batteries. And once again, as I lay there, that vile lassitude of mind and body stole over me. Actually I knew well I should be up and on after the retreating enemy in spite of shells, in spite of our own artillery fire, risking everything, so long as the enemy were kept on the move. But, I simply could not. Death hurtled past, bullets and shells, from the front only a hand's-breadth above me, from behind about twenty yards breadth to the left, but here I was sheltered from both directions, for the moment I was practically safe. What a relief, what comfort!

The men with us of the 52nd and of our own regiment, the 12th, smiled thankfully out of their grey-green faces, out of their still terror-stricken eyes, at us three officers: "Lucky we have the officers with us," said one: "Our's is such a silly fool he wouldn't know what to have done in that chimossel," said another.

"The captain will stay with us now?" asked one of the 52nd. "Our company officers were all killed on the ridge back there." Slightly abashed but none the less pleased with this unmerited confidence, I smiled back: "Yes, lads, we'll stick together now till the battle's over."

Time slipped by, was it a quarter of an hour, or an hour, or hours, I can't say! From in front, from behind, the storm remained unabated, as if mankind had usurped the powers of nature so great was the noise. Gradually, however, the picture changed. The little white whiffs of smoke to our left were no more and the music was different, we could hear the report of the discharges from the guns behind and the tearing scream of the shells as they passed overhead, but the noise of the bursts was no longer audible. The solution of this riddle was obvious; our artillery had at last tumbled to the fact that the enemy had gone and had lengthened their range accordingly. After a few minutes the enemy's artillery fire died down, the great concert, the colossal organ recital above our heads, ceased. We got up, stood upright, stretched out aching knees. I felt dizzy, giddy, almost intoxicated with exhaustion.

We had naturally lost touch with the enemy, and we now looked about us at the rows of miserable workmen's cottages with here and there small clumps of trees that seemed to have stayed by mistake in the midst of all this overgrown home of industry with its slag-heaps, mine-shafts, dirty sheds and buildings, and great chimneys with no flag of smoke waving from their tops. I had a feeling as if this second day of fighting – actually, God knows only of suffering for us, as my men had scarcely fired a shot – had taken place inside a gigantic factory.

"Come on, lads! Forwards, we must get touch again!" And we started off once more, trudged on in groups without any formation, haphazardly southwards through the chaos of conical slag-heaps, workmen's dwellings, sheds, and cabbage-patches, all now at peace again. Forwards! on through it all, trusting that we would find each other, find our own battalions, our own companies later as we went.

In a hollow by the side of a road stood a solitary house and on it the inscription: "Estaminet." Several field-grey gentlemen were standing outside the door. It drew us like magic, this distant smell of something to drink. And actually our intuition was correct. Up the dark steps leading from the cellar invisible hands handed up the most precious gifts of Paradise – bottles of all shapes and sizes filled with every kind of liquid. Like a big sponge, one's dried-up inside absorbed, lapped up every drop poured into it. Delicious, exquisite!

By degrees we began to sort ourselves out, to find our own places again. Large groups of my own company started to turn up led by NCO's or senior privates. My faithful staff too, Sauermann, Niestrawski, Pohlenz, somewhat ashamed of themselves. Today for the first time they had not kept by me. They protested it was not their fault. "It was like this, sir – " "Yes, lads, I'll believe you, you needn't tell me. But don't let it happen again."

I gathered together my own little army and we fell in with the column. The noise of battle had now ceased, only at times in the distance a rattle of musketry would begin and then as quickly die down again. We marched on southwards after the enemy and heaven knows how, but after a while the battalion was all together again, with the major at its head complaining that his adjutant, Lieutenant Stumpf, had been wounded. There, too, was von Reuter, our stern regimental commander. I reported to him that our own artillery had fired at us and caused us heavy losses. He thought for a moment, his face utterly unperturbed, and then answered quite calmly: "The Japanese artillery very frequently fired on their own infantry if they had advanced too rashly. They excused it by saying that it was better that the artillery fire should put out of action a few sections of their own infantry than that it should cease altogether for fear of doing so." So be it.

Adjutants flitted here and there and reorganised the wandering host into a semblance of order. After half an hour the entire regiment was assembled. A roll-call was taken by companies, and the losses were seen to be incomparably less than on the previous day. We had halted and piled arms near a factory that had been considerably damaged by shell-fire; the roof smashed in and a high iron shaft bent and splintered like matchwood. Again, by some miracle, the field-cookers were on the spot, and Ahlert, his face beaming all over, handed me a tin plate full of beautifully smelling soup. Good God! when was it – my last meal? Midday yesterday. I had eaten nothing for twenty-eight hours. Longer than that, surely, since our hurriedly finished meal in the village street at Baudour, eaten so innocently, so unsuspecting of what lay just ahead of us. It seemed an eternity.

The sun was already lowering in the cloudless August sky when we fell in again and marched on. The horses had come up and I now rode; glorious! to have one's tired limbs carried for one the rest of the day. The battle was over. We were march-ing on a good high road in column of fours, in perfect peace towards the south-west. For any who wished to talk there was plenty to talk about. Suddenly, rifle shots, bullets whizzed over the column. Yes! from that villa on the hill over there with the windows shuttered. The major told me to send a section against it. I de-tailed Sergeant Schiller. He extended his men, reached the house unopposed, and the fire from it ceased. Soon smoke and flames belched out from the windows and roof-tops, and whoever remained hidden inside would do no more harm.

Once again the march continued in profound peace, the peace of a summer evening all about us. Only here and there a column of smoke rising skywards, or an occasional gunshot in the distance. Now and again, lying in the ditch, was a dead man, stiff and staring, like a wax figure, a dying horse, a smashed-up bicycle, a bro-ken-down motor car. Many of the factories all around showed the marks of our shells, one of them also, very clearly, the skill of our enemy in the ways of war; the massive brick wall of the main building, itself proof against field artillery, had been loopholed all along to give accommodation for two batteries of guns.

We were all tired to death, and the column just trailed along anyhow. I sat on my war-horse like a bundle of wet washing; no clear thought penetrated my addled brain, only memories of the past two appalling days, a mass of mental pictures in-sanely tangled together that revolved eternally inside it. What had actually hap-pened since we left Baudour? None attempted to explain; a sad melancholy for all the dead friends seemed to pervade us all, strangely mixed with a hazy feeling of pleasure still to be in the land of the living oneself, still to be able to fill one's lungs with the air of a wonderful golden evening, still to be the master of one's weary limbs, still to feel a horse's back between one's legs.

It was already getting dusk as we entered a small town called, by the map, Dour. At first the inhabitants hung about down the side streets, evidently fright-ened, but as no one took any notice of them they came nearer and got into conver-sation. They said the English had gone through the place in crowds away to the south. We had halted in the market square under some trees and piled arms, every-one at once lying full length on the ground exhausted. Suddenly there was a com-motion as a car drove up into the square among us, bearing the flag of a general officer.

"Come round the car, everyone!" and standing upright in it was General Lochow, our Corps commander,[5] his ruddy face, with its small white moustache, looking fresh and vigorous. "Grenadiers!" he called out, "you have fought like ti-gers. You have shown the enemy so clearly what a Brandenburger can do that he has bolted, with his tail well between his legs. You will have seen, too, by the field-works they had made, that you were up against war-experienced, seasoned troops. In spite of that you have driven them out of all their carefully constructed defences, and sent them flying. In doing so you have had heavy losses yourselves, but you have added another victory to the famous colours of your regiment, a victory wor-thy to rank side by side with the immortal success of your fathers at Spicheren. I shall see to it that your deeds come to the notice of our Emperor and Commander-in-Chief, and he will be indeed proud of his Brandenburg Grenadiers. And now on to more battles ahead of us, to more victories, with three cheers for the Emperor! Hurrah! Hurrah! Hurrah!"

It was a full-throated shout from well-filled lungs such as I'd never heard nor joined in before; nevertheless, as the much-respected general waved his hand to us and drove away, we all looked at each other slightly disconcerted, almost shame-faced, mingled with our feelings of great elation. What! was that called a victory? Had we really won a big, important victory? Undoubtedly we had advanced ten miles southwards since our midday meal yesterday in Baudour, and the enemy who had tried to stop us had gone ... But otherwise the only impressions that remained in our dizzy brains were of streams of blood, of pale-faced corpses, of confused chaos, of aimless firing, of houses in smoke and flame, of ruins, of sopping clothes, of feverish thirst, and of limbs exhausted, heavy as lead. So that was victory! Amaz-ing! And yet it must be, the general had said so.

We sat for a long time in groups in the street on chairs brought for us out of their houses by the inhabitants. From a grocer's shop near by a pretty, laughing Belgian girl served us with chocolates, peppermints, and cigarettes, and the place was soon filled to overflowing with field-grey men, and completely sold out. It was dark before our billets were allotted. My company was given the schoolhouse, the sections fitting very comfortably into the big classrooms, whilst I and my senior NCO's, Sergeant Schüler and Esche, were given beds in the schoolmaster's house. Guarded by my new servant, Grychta (Zock had been absent since yesterday, whether dead or wounded no one could tell me), I got between sheets once more, and lying there I was filled with great emotion at the thought of having experienced my first real battle and being still alive. Yes, my beloved precious ones – I'm still alive. And in the deep silence of the night I gave thanks.

Chapter Twelve

At The Aisne

Very early the next morning we were again on the road, marching southwards towards the French frontier.

The enemy had vanished. The traces of a hasty departure, though not of a disorderly rout, were everywhere apparent: broken-down cars, burnt supplies, and so on, but no rifles or equipment lying about. The last two frantic days had been so full that I had not once taken the trouble to follow our course on the map, and so it was that we arrived close to the first objective of our march before realising it. A staff-officer, standing near a small house, called out to us:

"There, at the turnpike, is the French frontier!"

I rose in my stirrups and turned round to my company: "Do you hear that, lads! At this moment we are crossing the French frontier. Let's hope that before long we shall be crossing it again alive and well, and victorious – and homeward bound!" Loud rejoicing from the men. Again I had the feeling this was all a dream – fabulous.

The day was cooler, and a heavy shower of rain was most welcome after the stewing heat of yesterday. Strange how quiet the countryside had now become, the whole place silent as the grave. No more factories or tall chimneys, and the few villages absolutely and utterly empty, not a sign of a living soul. What on earth did these people imagine we were going to do to them? Heaven knows we had no wish to harm anyone who did none to us.

It was another long, weary march. To our left, away in the far distance, was a continuous boom like the long-sustained deep note of an organ mingled with the vibration of heavy muffled bells. What could it be? No doubt it was our heavy mortars which, having demolished Liège, were now bombarding Namur, about fifty miles away to the north-east. It was 11 pm that night before we reached our billets in the prosperous-looking village of Jolimetz. The battalion staff and B Company were allotted a very magnificent private house. As I was now the senior company commander, B Company automatically became the Headquarters Company, but after my experience at Glons I did not let the men sleep in the house; they had to erect their small tents in the cool of the garden and sleep outside. We officers had really delightful rooms, though the haste with which the owners had left them was apparent. The cellar, however, was princely in its capacity and contents. I got the company wagon up and filled it with all the bottles it had room for. I then told the other companies, who likewise took all they could carry, and still there was such a quantity left that I was able to offer it to the regiment. I would gladly have given requisition forms to the Mayor for all we had taken, but he and all his satellites, as all the rest of the inhabitants, had gone; this wealthy little place was completely deserted.

So deeply engrained in us was a sense of order and discipline that we began to feel like a dissolute band of mercenaries taking possession of these absent foreigners' houses and inviting ourselves to all the eatables and drinkables we could find in them, even though we were just as careful as if at home on manoeuvres. Nevertheless, it was with a sense of compulsory ownership that we sat down to dinner that evening round the Louis Seize dining table of our private house, and it was not often that such luxury came our way; for we drank the most exquisite Burgundy out of rich gilt tankards and then champagne from crystal wine-glasses. – Thank you, Mr So-and-so of Jolimetz! We then slept in the softest, most comfortable of beds for an all-too-short night.

On the road once more. Onwards! ever onwards! We passed through a large stretch of woodland, my company as artillery escort again, and on coming out of it there was a warlike interlude. The column was marching along the top of a ridge silhouetted against the skyline for many miles around. All of a sudden artillery opened on us from a distant wood, the shells hurtled just over our heads, whistling their now familiar tune and making that same revolting noise of some giant dog vomiting, as they burst and scattered their load of bullets on the house-tops on the right of the road. "Halt! Take cover!"

It was on occasional surprises such as these one noticed that the men, and oneself as well, were not as yet really steady under fire. A fear almost amounting to panic seemed to overtake the column, such as never occurred in the faintest degree in the middle of a battle. Our own guns soon silenced with a few rounds the impudent battery that had attempted to hold up our advance, and then on again, on – though not without a definite uneasiness in the ranks, the feeling that in these peaceful woodlands death might be lurking anywhere to jump out at any moment and take any one of us to its breast. This constant dread gave one's nerves no rest; it was, I found, one of the essential nerve-racking concomitants of war.

Throughout the day we heard incessant artillery fire away to our right, but during the midday halt news arrived that brought the blood back to our pale cheeks: Namur had been taken. The English and French armies in the north along the southern frontier of Belgium had been decisively beaten and were in full retreat. The Belgian army had withdrawn behind the forts of Antwerp. Our own corps during the past night had had another victorious engagement with the English, the 48th Regiment having annihilated all opposition.[1]

Bless my soul! it was like a fairy-tale. One victory after another. If it went on like this the war would be over in four weeks. A cautiously-minded voice warned us not to rejoice too soon. We might be able to see it through all right here in the West but … Yes, indeed! but the East, Russia's million army. One had heard nothing of it, absolutely not a word. As to what was happening there, not even the senior staff-officers were able to enlighten us.

A pitch-dark night again. Once more, as at Forst and Suerbempede, I was billeted under the roof of a Catholic priest, and was given a most friendly reception in this, the enemy's country. The priest was a good-looking young man in the late twenties, who carried on his work in the most modest poverty, his venerable mother acting as his housekeeper. He did all he could for the comfort of us worn-out, hungry warriors. Never shall I forget the picture as we all sat round the same table under a hanging oil-lamp; the handsome face of the priest, the snow-

1   Landrécies.

white head and wrinkled features of his little mother, and, side by side, five of my faithful "staff." Heavens alive, what a sight they were after three weeks of constant marching and fighting! Unshaved, and scarcely washed at all for days, their good-natured faces covered with a scrubby beard, they looked like prehistoric savages. Their coats were covered with dust and spattered with blood from bandaging the wounded, blackened with powder-smoke, and torn threadbare by thorns and barbed wire. The only thing respectable about them was their honest eyes, with which they did their best to express thanks to their host and hostess for a good meal, and they then listened most attentively, trying to understand the conversation in a strange language between their captain and the French priest and the nice-looking old lady.

When the regiment assembled the next morning, the 27th, we heard that the corps on our right, the Fourth, had won another battle against the English, who had made a stand at Le Cateau, and had captured twelve thousand prisoners and two batteries of guns. More rejoicing! Our march was now in a south-westerly direction in pursuit of the defeated English army, which had left traces of its hasty departure on all sides. Car after car in the ditch with burst tyres or broken axles, nearly all commercial vans with the names of private firms on them from apparently every big town in England, and containing, almost invariably, ammunition. England obviously regarded this war as a business undertaking and had collected all the transport resources of her private industries accordingly. Large heaps of supplies lay burnt by the roadside; the flames had destroyed the bread and any cereal food, but their only effect on the thousands of tins of Fray-Bentos bully-beef had been to cook the contents. It was excellent!

Our Rathenow Hussars were quick in discovering English stragglers. They brought whole squads of them out of farm buildings and houses, and a particularly favourite hiding-place was inside the cornstooks that lay piled all over the fields ungathered. The Hussars did not trouble to ransack every stook, but found that by simply galloping in threes and fours through a field shouting, and with lowered lances spiking a stook here and there, anyone hiding in them anywhere in the field surrendered. These stragglers were fine, smart young fellows, excellently equipped, but almost insolent in their cool off-handedness. As Sauermann said, "Every face wanted a warrant for arrest." The Hussars, unable to look after the prisoners themselves, handed them over to the infantry, and we took them along in the column with us until they could be handed over to a prisoners' collecting-station. At a longish halt a couple of Hussars came up to me: "Sir, we have taken prisoner a wounded English colonel and a major; they are in the waiting-room of the railway station over there; the major is un-hurt."

I went across and found two somewhat dishevelled but most gallant-looking gentlemen. Putting on my finest manners I greeted them in my best English and told them I had the honour to consider them as my prisoners – a turn in their career to which they appeared to resign themselves in a most cool and matter-of-fact manner. The major wore the ordinary infantry uniform with which I was now amply familiar, but the colonel had on a short khaki jacket, a dark blue schoolboy's cap with two long black silk bands hanging from it at the back, a short blue and black square-checked pleated skirt, between which and his stockings, which only reached to below the knee from a pair of brown shoes, was an expanse of muscular, hairy, naked leg. So he was a Scot, a Highlander.[2] I offered the elderly gentleman my arm, for he had had a bullet through his right shoulder and a ricochet hit on the knee that made him limp, and led him back to the company, who gazed at us in blank amazement. I requisitioned a horse and cart, and a farm-hand to drive it, from a farmhouse nearby, and asked the colonel to get up into it, and I placed my third horse at the disposal of the major; so kind and thoughtful we still were in those days to the English. Then I mounted my Belgian Alfred and the march continued.

Niestrawski came up alongside me almost bursting with indignation: "Please, sir, that's a dirty trick to play on anyone; surely our Hussars didn't do that – !"

"Didn't do what, lad?"

He thought for a moment, puzzled. "Or did those dirty swine actually take away their own wounded colonel's trousers?"

I almost wept with laughter. "No, my good fellow, the Tommies aren't quite as bad as that. The colonel belongs to a Highland regiment, he's a Scot – you'll see plenty of them in time. His checked ballet skirt, his stockings, and his naked legs are all part of the regulation uniform of Scottish regiments."

Niestrawski gaped at me open-eyed for a moment flabbergasted, then gradually a broad grin spread over his scrubby, bearded face, and he fell back giggling into the column again. A moment later he was explaining the affair to his friends: "The captain's made a grand joke: says the uniform of a Scottish Englishman is naked legs. Ha-ha-ha, great joke!" And the whole company shook with laughter at the wonderful wit of their captain.

That evening we billeted in the hamlet of Ponchaux, and it was an evening without compare for all of us. The first field-post arrived. Since the fourth day of mobilisation, that is for four weeks, four long weeks, I had had no word from home, and no one who has not had the same experience can understand to the full what the arrival of this first post meant to me, and to us all. Through all these days of toil and battle we had had no news whatever of what was happening there, and now suddenly came a whole pile of letters and parcels. If anyone had not realised before what home meant, what it was to have parents, or a wife and children to make one (and had any of us really appreciated it before as we did now?), then the past miserable weeks of privation must have taught us. It had been as if they were all dead and buried, as indeed they might have been, for all we knew. And now, I was actually holding her letters in my hand, some of them not a week old, my fingers trembling with suspense were opening the envelopes of the most recent, and already the opening lines had told me the news – that they were alive, all of them, and well. Tears ran down my haggard cheeks, my lips were pressed against the paper those loved hands had rested on only a few days since – and I, a hard-bitten, filthy dirty warrior, was not ashamed. Wretched exile I was, but how blessed, how fortunate.

Good heavens! What trouble they had taken in choosing things to send me, and what was I to do with all these cigars and cigarettes, the masses of chocolate, ginger-breads, tins of sardines, boxes of crystallised fruits, sweets; four weeks supply of them, all at once. But best, most welcome and important of all, were the letters.

2   A Gordon Highlander.

From my mother, a mother's benediction, one that I'd so missed before my departure, and from my children excited little epistles telling me all the strange upheavals the war had brought with it at home, how my boy kept watch at night for aeroplanes with a real loaded rifle under his arm, and my daughter told of a German lady my family had been asked to look after who with both her children had had to leave Paris at a moment's notice and had left behind them everything they possessed. And then my most beloved of all who is always, she writes, close to my heart. She complains of her terrible anxiety for me, prays that I am still unhurt, am still upright on both legs and that I may remain so, and have luck all through. Like a mother to her unruly son, she begs me to be careful, not to be too brave; not to expose myself unnecessarily to the bullets – ha, ha, ha! – my precious one, you darling! You can't know, then, how fond your big boy is of life, of this wild, terribly glorious thing called Life.

A few moments of the breath of home, away from the world, and then back to business to help the sergeant-major in the tragic task of sorting out the hundreds of letters and parcels that had to be returned home again, their recipients being already in some far-away hospital or, perhaps, in that mass-grave by the canal. This mournful job done, I tried to forget the sadness of it and plunged myself again with a purely selfish and exuberant joy among my treasures. How good they were, these cigars my mother had sent! Yes, mother, if only you could see your son at this moment; his scatter-brained youth gave you many a headache, but now at long last, after many days, he is deep immersed in the full tide of world-events.

We had got in exceptionally early on this day, after a march of only six miles; and when I went through the billets again to the temporary company office, to deal with a few minor offences, I scarcely recognised my worn-out, peevish, and utterly exhausted travelling companions. They were singing and laughing, smoking and feasting all over the place. Home, sweet home had come to them, just as it had to me, all the way across the great abyss of misery and horror that separated us from. it.

We celebrated that evening long and merrily in my billet; four of us, a captain and subaltern from a battery of heavy artillery, Sergeant Schüler, and myself. Schüler could not resist showing us the photograph he had just received of a slim Berlin girl to whom he was secretly engaged, and to whose health we all drank. Needless to say, we drank to the health of all our loved ones, and to those far-away beloved of my own I drank many, many times.

The "heavies" were not pleased with the way they had been employed up to date. "You have no idea what our guns can do. You rely only on the miserable 7.7 field gun, but if only we were given a chance you'd see something. There'd be dirty work at the crossroads, I can tell you."

It was not long before they were to have plenty of opportunity to show what their guns could do, and they were indeed to make dirty work at many crossroads.

Later, when I went to bed, I pressed to my heart that packet of letters from home. It was like a loved, caressing hand. Bless you, my precious ones!

The next day was a real griller; twenty miles under a blazing sun. One amusing incident relieved the monotony of the march during the afternoon. We were in the main body of the column, at the tail of the division, and had arrived west of Hancourt, on the main road, when suddenly the column halted; despatch-riders, adjutants, motor-cyclists flitted to and fro past us. We had heard artillery-fire in front, from the direction of the Somme, all day, and it was clear now that something was about to happen. While we waited an aeroplane with a black cross on it glided down, landing in a field to our left, and two young air-force subalterns very full of their own importance got out of it. They condescended to give us small scraps of information, scraps, nevertheless, that were full of hope. "Bülow's Army[3] was marching immediately east of us, and was making good progress; in a few days we should be in touch with it again …" Before we could draw any more wisdom from their young heads an order came to us: "Enemy's infantry advancing from the south. 1st Battalion, supported by Wiskott's Battery, will protect the left flank of the position, putting Beaumetz Farm in a state of defence." Orders were given out in feverish haste, the battalion deployed and the buildings and gardens of the large moated farm turned into a little fortress by a mass of panting men. We had practically finished; and were feeling that the enemy, so far as we were concerned, could now attack as much as he liked, when a staff officer galloped up: "For God's sake, don't fire! The column marching to south of us is the next corps!" (It was the Ninth, if I remember rightly.)

Feeling distinctly foolish we tidied the place up and fell in on the main road again to continue the march. Only B and C Companies, however, went on, for A and D were ordered to stay behind to guard an aeroplane landing-ground that was about to be cleared at the very place where our two young friends had come down. The major wrung his hands despairingly at losing half his battalion in this manner. *Vare, Vare, redde legiones!*

The soft evening light shed an almost tragic beauty over the country through which we now marched. The Fusilier battalion in front of us had, we heard, beaten off a French cavalry attack, and we were to be prepared to meet a possible rear-guard action of the retreating enemy, but nothing came of it. To our right, as we descended into the Somme valley, was Peronne, a mass of flame and smoke, the town looking like a gigantic torch in the dusk. In reality it was not so bad; but when, two years later, during the Somme battles, I came there again, the place had altered not a little!

It was about 9 pm when we reached a small hamlet, Le Mesnil-Breteuil, at the end of our tether. I had my billet in the house of an elderly woman who had remained to look after her home and her little garden, though her sons had fled. "Why should I run away? I know you people from the days of the 'Seventies. But now you look quite different – not nearly as handsome as then. You had blue coats with polished buttons in those days, and beautiful, shining helmets. Now you're grey all over, sad-looking – I don't like it."

She led me to a small room, my bedroom, and a strangely youthful smile lit up her wrinkled features as she spoke: "Well, captain, in the year 1870, when I was quite a young widow, a German army-doctor was billeted here for twelve days, and, believe me, I looked after him properly. I did all his washing, mended his clothes. I did every mortal thing for him, *tout, tout, tout, monsieur!* and all for love.

---

3   The German Second Army under General von Bülow was on this day about to engage with the French Fifth Army in the battle of St Quentin, about 18 miles east of Hancourt.

He was twenty-nine and I was twenty-five; in the afternoon he always used to sleep on the bed in his boots and spurs. There! You can still see the scratches of his spurs on the wood at the end of the bed," she giggled. "Oh, what a handsome fellow he was!"

It was with very mixed feelings that I went to sleep in this bed so rich in memories, and I wondered if he was still alive somewhere at home, this fortunate army-doctor of other days, and now perhaps a grandfather and a highly respected member of the medical profession.

Two days of continuous marching, the 29th and 30th of August, followed; it is difficult to describe the monotonous hardships endured in this incessant advance without any respite. Of the general situation, even of that of our own army,[4] the senior staff-officers one met appeared to know nothing. The so-called "common herd" which, as I heard a general say later in Russia, "in this war included everyone from a divisional commander downwards," had to be kept moving on like a flock of sheep and need be given no why or wherefore.

For three whole weeks, ever since we detrained at Elsdorf on August 10th, we had had not a single rest-day, nor even the suggestion of one. Day after day onwards without ceasing; every night in a fresh billet. The officers, it is true, had at least a bed and were able to take off their clothes at night; but the men throughout all this period of unspeakable trials and suffering had had only the straw they could pick up in the sheds and buildings to act both as mattress and blankets; they had had no time even to wash and dry their socks. Before the war I should have regarded such powers of endurance as beyond the capacity of the most robust peasant-lads; but since then I myself, in the autumn of 1915, as a battalion commander, neither took off my clothes nor saw a bed for seven weeks, sleeping entirely either in the open or in bare dug-outs – and I survived it. In pre-war days such hardships were never contemplated.

And how the men's feet suffered! From time to time we had to examine them; and it was no pleasure to look at the inflamed heels, soles, and toes of my wretched young lads, whole patches of skin rubbed off to the raw flesh. Many a morning we company commanders would ride up to the battalion commander: "Major, could you explain to the higher command the need for a rest-day? The men literally can go on no farther, and if we are asked to stand and fight any day now we cannot be responsible for their conduct under present conditions ..." The major shrugged his shoulders uneasily: "I assure you, gentlemen, I know all that as well as you do, and no day passes without myself and the other battalion commanders making this very same complaint to the colonel; but it seems quite useless. Apparently this frantic, everlasting onward rush is absolutely essential, and so you must keep on taking every care of your men on the march and use all your powers to keep up their spirits at any price. Make it clear to them that we must allow the enemy no rest until we have utterly defeated him on the whole front. Tell them that sweat is saving blood."

Yes, in that case there was nothing else to do but to use all one's powers to keep the men's tails up. We explained what we could to them, and they were grateful.

I should have to quote a thousand and one little details to show how the privations we were enduring day by day gradually brought together the officers and their

---

4   The First Army under General von Kluck, forming the right of the German battle-line.

men in a common bond of fellowship. Gradually one was getting to know the name of every man in the company, his trade in civil life, and his special qualifications, and it became an ever-increasing pleasure and happiness as our acquaintance with each other improved. I did not find one single really bad character among them. There were a few rather worthless fellows whom one tried to make something of; but the chief mischief was the propensity to add on all possible occasions to the scanty rations given to them by independent requisitioning. It was, however, only human that the soldier should take what he badly needed – and his growling stomach told him that clearly enough – and which he found at his hand left behind by the owner. Those were the very natural feelings of the soldier, and it was difficult to prevent him acting on them.

The 30th August brought us an important bit of news: a change in the direction of our march, a new strategical objective. The full meaning of it is not even yet clear to me, as it would need a fundamental study of the campaign, which only the history of the war will unfold. Nevertheless, since crossing the Belgian frontier into France we had been marching in a fairly straight south-westerly direction, the prolongation of which by Montdidier, Beauvais, and Gisors would have taken us considerably westwards of Paris. Now, we were to turn suddenly east-wards through Bouchoir to Parvillers and thence in a south-south-easterly direction which at first appeared to be taking us direct on Paris itself, and later more and more to eastward of it. It meant in any case that the whole (First) Army was making practically a complete right wheel.

The general reason was explained to us something as follows: General Bülow's (Second) Army is heavily engaged on our left, and will shortly completely smash the resistance of the enemy opposing it. Our object now is to continue to drive the beaten enemy southwards as before, but also to force him away from Paris, and at the same time, by forced marches, to cut off the enemy now opposing Bülow's Army from his roads of retreat on Paris, and, if possible, surround him.

That all sounded very sensible: it also gave a perfectly sound reason for the continuation of these incessant marches regardless of the suffering to be endured. So it was that on the following day, the 31st, we were given an example of what was expected of us. On the 30th we had only done 18 miles; but on this day, the first in the new direction, we accomplished 28 miles in blazing sun all day. Nor was it a straightforward march, for several interruptions occurred. As we were assembling, and while it was still dark, a staff-officer, Major v M, came up and told me most favourable news of the general situation, the best of all being that all was going well on the Eastern Front. The Russians had apparently advanced well into East Prussia, ravaging the place wherever they went; but in the past few days the position had altered decisively. A big battle had taken place in the district of Gilgenburg-Ortelsburg, in which the Germans, commanded by a certain von Hindenburg, had completely annihilated the Russian Army of the Narew and taken over 60,000 prisoners.

We passed through the lovely old town of Roye, and, although we only marched through the outer streets of it, a halt there enabled us to enjoy a glimpse of its wonderful old Gothic cathedral. We were, in fact, now passing through a district full of world-famous architectural beauty, but all too quickly to see it properly. This was a suffocating day: thank goodness, I had a horse to ride! Early in the afternoon we reached the swampy, wooded valley of the Oise, and were to cross it near Ribecourt. The main bridge had been blown up, but, inexplicably, a small suspension bridge had been left in position. It was narrow and swayed dangerously; only one cart or one gun could be on it at a time, so naturally there was a long delay.

We had scarcely got across before an order arrived: "The crossings over the Aisne at Attichy are to be secured today at all costs, and also, if possible, the main road Soissons-Compiègne."

The 1st Battalion on this day was the rear battalion of the advanced guard; and when we had crossed a second branch of the Oise at Bailly it was found that, owing to, the delays, a big gap now existed between us and the battalions in front, the Fusilier and 2nd Battalions, who had already gone on with all speed to the Aisne. Here, after a short fight with English cavalry patrols and with the inhabitants,[5] they had crossed the river, occupied the railway station on the far side, and torn up the rails.

On this day the two companies we had left to guard the new aeroplane landing-ground near Beaumetz Farm rejoined us, so the battalion was now complete once more. In the dusk we marched through the picturesque village of Tracy-le-Mont and thence through the northern part of the Forest of Compiègne on to a bare plateau, where late in the evening we bivouacked near a lonely farm, called La Falaise. After a day of such burning heat the night was so mild that the men did not trouble to put up their bivouac tents, and simply spread out the unthrashed straw from the farm over the ground to sleep on. It was a beautiful, though melancholy, picture this bivouac on the bare, lonely hill in brightest starlight with burning flames reaching skywards away to the south, the first we had seen since leaving Belgium. I slept with the battalion-staff on straw in a small shed.

The next morning we were early astir, and marched down to the Aisne valley. At the entrance to Attichy a big farm lay in smouldering ruins; and I remembered the report of the previous day that the inhabitants had taken part in the fight here: this was the result. It was the only case I noticed in French territory. In the village itself the German field post-office was already established, the first I had seen. Up till now the only chance of getting a letter back home had been to give it to any passing mounted orderly to post where he could. Now at last the letter-box was within reach; but no writing-paper, no envelopes, only the official field-postcards with their dull formula, and these dated back to the years 1870–71! Oh, blessed German economy!

In the middle of the village was a signpost:

"Paris 50 Kilometres."

It pointed in the direction we were marching; that is, across the Aisne to the great high road which followed the course of the river southwards. We had not the slightest doubt that we were to follow it too. The French Government, we heard, had left Paris and gone to Bordeaux. Paris itself, so said the rumours that were constantly running up and down the column, had been declared an open town, and no

---

5   Rearguard patrols of the 3rd Cavalry Brigade (4th Hussars, 5th Lancers, 16th Lancers) covering the retirement of the II Corps.

attempt was to be made to defend it by its forts, in order to save it from the fate of Liège and Namur.

And now we were only thirty miles from the City of Light; thirty miles, that meant two days' march at most at our present rate of progress: so that by tomorrow evening at latest we would be standing at its gates, and perhaps the following morning make our triumphal entry into the surrendered city.

How vividly at this time the memories came back to me of the unforgettable months I had spent in Paris three years before, in 1911, when working on my play *Volk wider Volk*. I seemed to enter so completely into the life of that wonderful town, and found so many friends there, that I had become in my heart a good Parisian citizen. And now, maybe, the day after tomorrow I was to enter it as a conqueror, sitting on my war-horse at the head of my grey company. No, it's not possible! It's all a dream. And, in truth, that part of it was to remain a dream ...

The regiment was still advanced guard, and as we had retained the order of yesterday our battalion was again at the tail, behind the artillery. As we crossed the Aisne valley we could overlook the long column in front as it moved on southwards towards a railway embankment ahead. I was riding by the side of my former subaltern, von der Osten, who since Tertre had been commanding A Company.

"Look, Osten," I said, "that's the main road to Compiègne and Paris, just beyond the railway embankment over there! Soon you'll see the point of the advanced guard turn to the right along it." I showed him the place on my map – my map, because he hadn't one. Since Roye, in fact, we had been off our official maps: on mobilisation we had only been issued with maps of Belgium and Northern France, and so rapid had been our advance that sufficient maps of Central France had not been sent forward, with the result that only battalion commanders had them. For two days we company commanders had been riding on into an unknown world without maps. For myself, however, my faithful Ahlert had produced a French motoring-map from some broken-down car by the wayside, which was for the time being a valuable and much-coveted treasure. I had to thank it for all the knowledge I was displaying.

"But look, sir!" said Osten a few moments later. "The advanced guard is not turning to the right. They're going straight on."

"What? Surely, you don't mean –," and then I saw he was right. Our noses were no longer leading to Paris. They led us on due south, and crossed at right angles the great high road to the City of Light.

Shortly afterwards came a regimental order: "Enemy infantry and cavalry in position on the high ground at Taillefontaine. The regiment will attack. Fusilier battalion will take up a preparatory position immediately west of Roy-St Nicholas: 2nd Battalion on its right and in touch with it: 1st Battalion in support behind the 2nd."

We racked our brains for some explanation that would not dash our hopes of the triumphal entry, and soon found one. Of course, it was obvious. A weak force of the enemy had been reported to southward, and it was naturally the duty of the advanced guard to clear them away and occupy the high ground, while the division passed on. It would doubtless send out another advanced guard and continue its march along the great high road to Paris. There might be a small fight here, and then we would follow on after the division, arriving possibly half a day later in Paris.

We passed through a wooded defile. Above us the deployment for attack was being carried out as ordered, and then the advance began, we, the 1st Battalion, moving in column of sections in support. Not a shot was fired anywhere, the enemy must have decamped before we arrived. During a short rest in Taillefontaine village on the high ground, Corporal Fischer, my hard-worked requisitioning-officer, made a great find. He came up to me beaming; he had discovered no less than seventy-five loaves of good white bread in the cellar of a baker's shop! I immediately sent two groups under Corporal Esche to stake our claim and take possession.

At this very moment came the order to move, and, what was worse, the 1st Battalion was now to lead the advanced guard. Worse still, my company was the leading company of the battalion, and had to send out a point, and the leading section was Esche's.

I let the section go on under a corporal, as Esche was still down in the baker's cellar. Every other man of the section already had under his arm an enormous French roll of bread over a foot long and half a foot across.

"For God's sake, lads, hide away the bread under the flap of your packs as you go along!"

I trotted on to the end of the village to have a look at the country beyond; and in the meantime young Esche with the rest of his section had come up from the cellar and found neither his men nor his rifle, which another had taken on for him. However, being a hungry young man of nineteen years, he was blissfully happy with his foot of fresh, white bread, and he ran on after his section, the big roll under his arm. Just as he reached it, the leading section, the point of the advanced guard, he suddenly saw General Sontag, the brigadier, standing just in front by the roadside. He now completely lost his head. Instead of getting his rifle and handing over the bread, he placed himself at the head of his section – the leading man, if you please, of the leading company of the advanced guard of the First Army of His Excellency General von Kluck! – without a rifle, and in its place a gigantic roll of bread under his arm – and behind him his eight men still making spasmodic efforts to stuff their own rolls away under the flaps of their packs.

The brigadier was aghast, utterly dumbfounded, and shouted to Esche in a voice of steel: "Who is your company commander?"

"Captain Bloem, sir."

"Where is he?"

"I – don't know, General."

"The captain has ridden on ahead, sir – there he is by those trees!" called out one of the section.

"Go and bring him here, Zerboni," the general said to his adjutant. "Halt! you miserable lot of idiots!" to Esche and his section.

The adjutant fetched me, and the general received me in a towering rage. "What the devil does this mean, all this damned tomfoolery!" In a few moments the affair was put right, the bread was stowed away, and Esche had his rifle again. "Now march on, Esche," I said quietly.

The general allowed me to explain, and then the fury on his face cleared away. He laughed and I laughed too, irresistibly.

"When you write your next war-book, Bloem, don't forget to describe the way in which you allowed your company to march when you had the honour of leading the advanced guard of the army."

"Right, General! I won't forget." And now I wish to report, most respectfully, that I have carried out your order, General.

The march continued and was a harassing one. After a few minutes rifle bullets whistled past out of the woods on our right and left. A Hussar from one of the cavalry patrols ahead lay dying by the roadside close to his horse, also breathing its last. The firing became worse as we went on, for the woods came nearer to the road and finally closed in on it at both sides. I told off two sections to go through the strip of wood on the right side of the road whilst a troop of Hussars set off to do the same on the left. We passed a most unpleasant hour, until finally the woods had been cleared.

In the village of Heraumont there was a long halt. I rode forward to reconnoitre and noticed in a side street two splendid horses haltered to a garden-fence. My experience at Tertre and Louvain with captured horses had taught me a lesson. The six English horses I captured at the beginning of the battle of Tertre, when I had my duel with the cavalry sergeant-major, had been annexed with great pleasure by the brigade staff when they were taken back. This time I would be more careful and keep them myself.

Naturally, where horses are, there are also riders. "Schüler," I said, "take a couple of strong men of your section into the house with you and have a look round." A few moments later he returned and reported that an English colonel lay dying inside, with an English doctor attending him, and that the horses belonged to them. A little later the doctor appeared and was brought to me, a look of cool indifference on his clean-shaven face. He said the colonel, a battalion commander, had just died. The doctor then reported to Major von Kleist, who decided that under the rules of the Geneva Convention he should not be treated as a prisoner, but be kept with us until we had an opportunity of handing him over to look after English wounded prisoners. He was content. I let him have his own horse, and told him to consider himself as my guest for the time being. So kind were we still to the English!

We halted at midday on a bare hillside and the cookers came forward. To our right was the ancient, out-of-the-world village of Largny, and to our left an endless view of wooded hills and dales. In the middle of the meal two shrapnel suddenly hurtled above our heads and burst in the village gardens. Just two, no more and no less. Heaven knows what the enemy fired them for. A report came in: "Enemy column of all arms marching westwards from Villers-Cotterets." At once all was in movement again. The 1st Battalion was advanced due south with the Fusilier battalion on its right, the 2nd Battalion in support. We crossed some high ground into a valley beyond which the company extended, and then climbed the thickly wooded southern slope, troublesomely steep. As we reached the top the first shrapnel burst over us. The enemy[6] shot with amazing and consistent accuracy, the bullets clattering into the trees just above our heads at each burst. So long as we kept down just below the steep bank on top they went over us; but if one raised one's head above it, the lead rattled about one's, ears: rifle bullets, too, as we could hear by their noise.

I called Schüler, and told him that we should have to advance about 150 yards into the open, as the wood-edge where we were gave the enemy's guns too easy a target. I asked him to go forward himself first and choose a suitable place for a firing-line. He doubled out with the utmost coolness to the distance I'd ordered, knelt down and examined the field of fire, then returned and led his section to the line in three rushes. I joined them. We now lay in the open field, and by the faint haze of smoke near some trees in front were able to gauge roughly the position of the enemy's guns, which continued to burst their shells along the wood-edge we had left. I gave the section an aiming mark, estimating it to be at 1600 yards range, and we opened fire. The shelling began to slow down, and I ordered up the rest of the company to line out, one man being killed and another wounded in the rush across the open.

A small procession of fine guinea-fowl walked in single file across our front over the stubble: being a townsman I only recognised them by having met them in the Zoological Gardens. Now and again they attempted to fly: some flew into our bullets, others got higher among the enemy's shells and down they came, all of them being soon either dead or fluttering helplessly about the field.

On my right I suddenly heard Pohlenz's voice: "Here are some cigars, sir!" He handed them along to me, a handsome case with ten cigars in it, marked with the name of an English tobacconist. I distributed them to right and left. Thank you, Tommy, my friend! We came to the conclusion the cigars must have fallen out of one of the shells bursting above our heads: often and often during the battles to come I was asked: "Why aren't the enemy shooting with cigars again today?"

This fight lasted about an hour, and then the enemy ceased fire and moved off. It was already dusk, and after a cross-country march through swamps, hedges, and barbed-wire fences the regiment at last assembled in Coyolles, already filled to overflowing with troops and wagons, and then marched on down a steep hill to billets in the quiet, peacefully slumbering village of Vauxiennes. There followed the usual nightly performance of allotting the houses and sheds to companies and breaking down the locked doors with axes.

I and my guest, the English doctor, had a miserable room in a labourer's cottage. I gave up half my bedding for my "staff" to lie on on the floor, and we passed the night all of us quite comfortably and the best of friends. The Englishman wrote a letter to his wife, which I had posted for him. He let me read it first: "My sweetheart, I am now with the Germans, but you need have no anxiety about me, as I am being very well treated and get plenty to eat, and there are fewer bullets here than with us. Your own Fred."

The next morning, the anniversary of Sedan, the march was continued through a large forest. From. Boursonne onwards the regiment was responsible for guarding the division from any attack from the south: the 1st Battalion was advanced guard, my company being again leading company. I had scarcely given my orders and sent out the point when the regimental staff trotted past and rode right on quite casually up the hill in front. I went to Major von Kleist, the battalion commander: "Major, do you see that? It's all wrong. Supposing, as yesterday, there are a few English stragglers, or a patrol, in the wood, they will shoot the colonel and his staff straight away. Won't you ride ahead and ask him to keep to his place at the head of the main body behind?"

The major shrugged his shoulders: "I'll try, but he'll only laugh at me for my trouble." And so it was. I could see from where I was the indifferent gestures of the colonel as they spoke together. "What did he say, major?"

"He says the road through the forest is difficult, and as he was responsible for the safety of the division he was going to lead himself." There was nothing more to be said, and so it was that we marched through a forest in the enemy's country in the following order: First came Colonel von Reuter and his staff, then the battalion commander and myself, then a cavalry patrol followed finally at the regulation distance by the point of the advanced guard and my company. That was the sort of person our colonel was, and yet no harm came to him.

Soon we were crossing the last ridge that separated us from the Marne valley. It was another grilling, exhausting day. Twenty-five miles up hill and down dale under a blazing sun. To our left we could hear the guns of Bülow's Army with which we seemed to be nearly in touch again.

It was pathetic to see the endless mass of refugees fleeing madly in continuous streams along all the roads leading south, trying to escape from us. And now the roads were blocked ahead they could get no farther. Always the same ever-recurring little family tragedy: a cart with railed sides packed high with furniture and belongings, and drawn by miserable, broken-down horses: lying somewhere among the belongings an old man, fainted with the heat or with sunstroke, or an elderly woman pining away with worry, and the family, men, women, and children, half-starved, exhausted, dirty and neglected, shambling along literally trembling at the sight of us and the fear of being killed.

Oh, all you journalists of Brussels, Lille, St Quentin, and Paris, you slandering propagandists and preachers of hate, do you realise what suffering you caused your own countrymen by the unscrupulous string of lies and base gossip with which you filled your papers in those days, and what a mass of homes, health, and life you destroyed by your deceit?

The sun was beginning to set, when suddenly, spread out at our feet, was a picture of indescribable loveliness: the valley of the Marne. There was such a charm in its lazy atmosphere of serene unruffled peace that we greeted thankfully the order to halt, and we lay on the grass by the roadside struck dumb with the beauty of the scene. Immediately beneath us was the railway, shining threads of silver in the sunlight, and I recollected that, three years ago, it was here along these rails that I had returned from Paris. If anyone had told me then ...

Only a few moments of these dreamy memories, for suddenly on the left, about ten miles off, artillery fire boomed into the peace of the valley, and then away to the south, like a flock of white sheep moving in line across the blue evening sky, one saw the little white clouds of the shrapnel-bursts from Bülow's guns.

A cavalry squadron in front had already crossed the bridges, and our 2nd Battalion pushed on past, with the ridge on the far side of the valley as its objective. We marched on down and through the old country-town of Nanteuil. Not a soul in the streets but here and there a terror-stricken face peering through the shuttered windows. On the bridge were some of our cyclists: one of them, full of merriment, said to me: "We had great; fun, sir! When we got to the bridge, people came up to us and asked: 'Anglais? Anglais?' and as our lieutenant had told us always to say 'oui, oui, oui,' we said 'oui, oui, oui.' Then the people brought us a mass of stuff to eat and drink and put flowers in our buttonholes. But when our cavalry came up the people realised we were not English but Germans. They screamed and ran away in all directions, but it didn't matter; we'd got all we wanted!"

And then we crossed the Marne. On the far side we halted awaiting the order for billeting. Never shall I forget that evening. The firing to our left had ceased. The sun had sunk into a misty haze of deepest gold. The whole valley, steeped in the perfect stillness of a summer evening, shimmered in the golden light. Could this be war? Could anyone fight here? Impossible. It was peace on earth, the peace that passeth understanding.

On such an evening one's thoughts inevitably flew homewards. Since Ponchaux, a week ago, we had had no further post, no news, though the scraps we had were all good. The news of the great victory on the Eastern front had been confirmed: as for Paris, we were already level with it, and behind us there would certainly be reserves following on who would be extending our line away to the west and might already be in the heart of the capital. And tomorrow Bülow would be enveloping the remnants of the French Army opposing him. In a couple of weeks the campaign would be over. Just like a fairy-tale!

We went into billets in Citry, a quiet little village in the valley. I now had another company-officer, Lieutenant Chorus, who since Tertre had been commanding "C" Company, now taken over by Count Westarp. "A" Company also now had a new commander, Captain von Bülow of the 11th Grenadiers, who had till now been with the general staff. He arrived a very elegant staff-officer, shaved, washed, and well turned-out; in a few days he had acquired the same bristly, dirty appearance as the rest of us.

Once more a comfortable French farm-house welcomed us as guests as hospitably as if we'd been on manoeuvres in our own country. The farmer's wife, a fine woman, brought us a meal of boiled eggs, baked potatoes, beautiful golden-yellow butter, and most delicious cider: she told me, with tears in her eyes, that her husband had joined the Territorials, and that her five sons and her son-in-law had joined the army.

"And yet, madame, you treat us as if we were your defenders and not your enemies?"

"Well, sir, I think like this: what I am doing now for you, I hope, perhaps, some other mother will be doing for my poor young men."

I wonder if she still thinks the same, or has the hatred of us, so artfully and maliciously propagated the world over, eaten too deep into her brave and honest heart? or has the grief for the death of one or perhaps more of her sons dried up that great spring of human love within her?

Chapter Thirteen

The Marne

From now on we were almost continually in action.

The following morning, September 4th, we crossed the high ground that separates the Marne valley from that of the Petit Morin. On the way I had rather a heated row with my company. I had constantly forbidden them to take food from the houses without permission, and that was the cause of the trouble. The supply columns from the rear seldom reached us, and we still lived on the country, so that the daily rations were often sketchy. The company butchers, Elberling and Liebsch, working day and night in the most difficult circumstances – only getting a few hours' rest out of the twenty-four – were able to maintain a sufficient supply of meat. I can never picture these two splendid youngsters other than with rolled-up sleeves, their arms red to the elbows, and their jackets and trousers covered with blood and bits of fat: they often had to cope with a very mixed bag: a pig, a calf, a goat, half a dozen chickens, a few rabbits, all thrown into the field-cooker together – a witch's cauldron. Nevertheless, it was not sufficient: the most important, the only really satisfying ingredient was missing, and that was bread. Undergoing great physical strain, the men needed ample food and were taking all that they could find; but that was against orders, which were particularly strict on this point. The consequent tendency to a lack of discipline had to be checked at all costs.

A little later rifle-fire was opened on the advanced guard, and a message arrived: "Bellot is occupied by the enemy. The regiment will attack ... 1st Battalion in support."

The Fusilier and 2nd Battalion, who were in front, stormed. the village and took a number of prisoners. We, the 1st Battalion, were not engaged except for toiling through a wood filled with dense undergrowth and a mass of bullets whizzing about us. We marched through the village that was seething with French wounded and prisoners, and then up a narrow valley to Grand-Doucy. Here we had the midday halt in a shady orchard close to the road full of the most luscious pears, and grapes in abundance. My company did justice to them, and all got their fair share, even the captain! All the same we were none of us quite at our ease, for, as Sauermann remarked, the whole place smelt of the enemy. And he was right. Our midday rest, given out to be for two hours, was abruptly cut short after half an hour. "The villages to the south, Champ Martin and St Barthélemy, occupied by a strong force of the enemy. The regiment will attack!"

We had scarcely started off again, still in the village, when an artillery duel started, the enemy's shells bursting at the end of the street in front. Moving on we passed a stream of wounded men from the Fusilier battalion going back covered with blood. We then deployed for the attack on Champ Martin, but lost touch with the battalion in front, and so, going on on our own initiative, we found the village already in the hands of the Fusilier battalion, which had lost heavily in getting it. In the village the companies, which had become mixed up in the advance, reorganised, and then we moved on again to attack St Barthélemy. The shells from our own guns were already screaming over our heads into the village, and the enemy must have evacuated it straight away, for we entered it unopposed. It was astounding to see how much damage had been done to it by only a few minutes' bombardment.

Another order: "A strong column of enemy cavalry advancing from the northwest: 1st Battalion will occupy the outer edges of the village facing the enemy." The battalion order on this was: "B, C, and D Companies will dig in along the edge of the village; A Company and Battalion Headquarters will remain by the church."

So that was to be the reward for a hot day's march; we were to spend the night in an entrenched position; for the first time, a night in the trenches, or rather in what we were then pleased to call trenches. It is difficult now to imagine what an intense, deep-rooted aversion the German soldier had to the spade in those early days of the war. One almost had to put the spades into their hands before they would start to dig, and when they'd got down a couple of feet they considered that more than sufficient.

It was getting dusk, and so I sent patrols out in front, still feeling it as a reproach to myself to send gallant fellows off into the unknown and stay behind. On the southern horizon we could see clearly with the naked eye the main road leading from Milleray to La-Ferté-Gaucher, and along it tiny silhouetted shapes were continually moving westwards; now a little group on foot, now a few on horseback, now a gun, now a few baggage wagons ...

"Will you go on with your digging, lads! What's happening over there doesn't concern you. I'll look after that!"

Müssigbrodt came up to me with a broad grin; he had put the horses in one of the nearest farms, and now asked me to go back with him a moment as there was something worth seeing. As I entered the farm, an old peasant came up ringing his hands: "Oh, sir! it's terrible, terrible! I'm a poor man and I'm done. It's all over! Oh, help me, sir!"

"Well now, what's happened?" He pointed to the house, and I saw that a shell had torn a great hole through the front wall, crossed the sitting-room, gone clean through a cabinet of china against the back wall, and there it had stuck unexploded, enormous, and unashamed, firmly fixed in the wall, with the pile of debris it had caused beneath it.

"Take it away, sir! Oh, please sir, take it away!"

"Not likely, old man. Let it stay quietly where it is, and show it to your children's children as a memory of the Great War."

"Oh, sir, impossible! I shall die of fright – have pity on me, sir!"

"Nothing doing. Good-night, papa!"

I had only been back a few minutes at the trench, broadening and deepening very, very slowly, when all at once a mad firing started on the left beyond C Company where the machine-gun company had dug in.

"Hullo, what's up!" It was a cavalry attack. We could see, coming out of a wood, two or three dozen riders in steel helmets and blue overcoats moving towards the front of the next company, followed by more and still more. Our machine guns swept them, and one after another they fell from their horses; here and there a horse would rear up on its hind legs and collapse, while others rushed on past us as if ridden by devils. It was soon over; surely the enemy had gone mad.

Fifteen minutes later a cyclist brought a message for me to go to the market square in the village to see the major. I went back through the dark, narrow street. In the middle of the square was the church, and from an upper window a faint light showed up a red-cross flag flying from it. Wounded were being brought or dragging themselves to it from every direction, German and enemy all together. Nearby, in an open space in the square, sat the major, a flickering candle at his side. Around him in a circle lay and stood a dozen or more French cuirassiers, most of them badly hit, and their wounds wretchedly bandaged with bloody pieces of rag. Major von Kleist was struggling to remember his French grammar, but in vain.

"Awful, Bloem, isn't it? Will you cross-examine these prisoners? They speak a language I simply can't understand." In a few minutes I had unravelled the mystery of the cavalry attack. The cuirassiers had been with a baggage column which had lost its way and had suddenly come under fire from our machine guns. I asked whence they had come and where going, but could get little out of them; like good soldiers they held their peace. "We were on the march westwards, captain, always westwards. What is happening elsewhere, how the battle is going, we have no idea, we know nothing, absolutely nothing!"

The prisoners were led away, though one of the seriously wounded the major, in the goodness of his heart, ordered to remain. "Take him into one of the houses still inhabited, and let him be looked after by his own countrymen. The poor fellow can do no more harm."

I returned "home" through the dark, empty village streets, that is, to where I belonged, to my company. It was a starlight night of darkest, deepest blue. I bedded down in the trench between Sauermann and Niestrawski, for it was now broad enough to take three men abreast, lying breast to back. Pohlenz, curled up like a hedgehog, lay at our feet.

And in this way, surrounded by my faithful "staff," I spent my first night in the trenches.

To any of us who had not yet noticed it, the events of the past days must have shown how increasingly unpleasant the situation was becoming. We had, indeed, achieved marvels, driving the enemy out of the whole of Belgium and a great part of Northern France, nevertheless we ourselves were getting farther and farther away from home with ever-lengthening communications, while more and more enemy were now appearing on our front; they seemed to be everywhere, chiefly cavalry, it's true, nevertheless they were all about us. What could it mean? I think we all felt considerable uneasiness at this period, though we kept silent on the subject; no one would have dared do otherwise.

We marched down from the high ground the next morning into another valley through which flowed the Grand Morin. Again the ridge on the far side was held by the enemy, and again the order to attack; once more, too, the 12th Grenadiers were in front. The regiment deployed, and we struggled through another typically French wood, utterly neglected and covered with a dense undergrowth. On reaching a clearing the fire from the wooded slope opposite was so persistent that I ordered the company to fire a few rounds at random into it, the actual enemy position being invisible. Then we went on and, while crossing a flat meadow in the bed of the valley, stood of a sudden at the edge of a steep bank with a fast-running stream, eight yards wide, at our feet. Near by appeared to be a footbridge, but on closer inspection it was two long, slender fir trees laid across with narrow bars a yard apart and no rail. To walk over it would have been a skilled acrobatic performance with the risk of a soaking in the stream, and the only alternative was to crawl. Getting down on all fours I scrambled across to the far side mostly flat on my stomach, with bullets flicking about me, and then the company followed man by man, extending out into the field on arrival. As soon as one section was across it advanced and began to ascend the wooded slope, but before the whole company was over the enemy had gone; a mass of cartridge cases, broken branches, and trampled ground alone remained.

The regiment reassembled in a village and the march continued to Pierrelez, where we had the midday rest near a half-ruined Gothic church, now a barn. The cookers came up and gave us our usual meal; scraps of meat, killed only a few hours before, and a sort of soup made in pots which, by the smell, had obviously not been cleaned for many days: there was no time for such details! The artillery, which had been delayed by the blown-up bridges over the Grand Morin, now picked us up.

Another message: "Two enemy infantry battalions are marching along the southern edge of the wood on Sancy,[1] which is occupied by the enemy." Naturally we were to attack. Very fine and very glorious, but in the long run it was beginning to play hell with our nerves and our tired bones.

This time the 2nd and Fusilier battalions had the honour of leading the dance. They deployed, and their skirmishing lines soon disappeared among the trees to the south. Soon afterwards a rattle of musketry started. We, the 1st Battalion, piled arms and lay down on the right of the main road that ran through a slight cutting here on its way southwards to Sancy-les-Provins. We watched the machine-gun company and a battery of artillery go past and disappear into the deep shadows of the wood; also a number of staff-officers trotted past and, finally, even the Divisional commander, General Wichura, in his car.

Lying flat, we listened to the spasmodic crackle of rifle-fire in front. This too would probably fizzle out like the others, one thought, when suddenly there was a great uproar in front like a burst of thunder, a volcanic eruption, and floating above the wood appeared more flocks of white sheep in long lines coming from nowhere and apparently harmless, yet shedding their dung of black bullets all over the place. And now a dozen more – just over our heads. "Stand to!" I shouted to my company from the opposite side of the cutting, simultaneously with the other company commanders. But it was unnecessary, for all had seen it, and in a flash they had slipped on their packs and unpiled their rifles. The road was evidently the aiming mark of the enemy gunners, and we must get away from it at once. "Into the wood, everyone! Sections assemble a hundred yards on!"

Scarcely had the majority of the company got away before a salvo of shells burst on the road within a few yards of where they had been lying a minute before. A mass of smoke, dirt, stones, and splinters rose in the air. I was still half-stunned by this explosion within a few paces of me, when a frantic tumult took place in the

---

1   Troops of the French Fifth Army (General Franchet d'Esperey) retiring immediately east of the British Expeditionary Force.

wood – the clattering of horses' hoofs at racing speed, the rattle of wheels, and above it all cries and shouts of agony. A cloud of dust came towards me along the road and in the midst of it the galloping legs of horses, their foaming mouths slavering blood.

It was clear what had happened. The sudden burst of shell-fire had hit and caused a panic in the machine-gun company and the battery; the horses, mad with fright and pain, had swung round and bolted ... Already the mass was tearing past me in its wild career, the machine-guns all awry on their broken limbers, the guns of the battery making frenzied bounds behind the rocking limbers, the gunners blood-spattered and their faces distorted with terror clung desperately to their seats, until one after another they rolled off into the dust and under the hoofs of the satanic stampede ... There, too, was the car of the Divisional commander, the wind-screen smashed, and in it the general himself, calm but pale as a statue. The procession romped and flickered past my astonished eyes, while behind a second and third volley of shrapnel burst on the road.

It was time I joined my company. Taking advantage of a gap in the cavalcade of horror I crossed the road in three long strides, being squirted with hot blood from the open artery of a dying horse on the way, and then ran on to the wood, to find my lads agitated beyond measure and still staring open-mouthed at the road of much misery.

"You're bleeding, sir! The captain's wounded ..."

I had to laugh in spite of all. "Don't worry, lads, it's only horse's blood, not mine." But in my innermost self I felt my hair standing on end and my knees still shaking.

After a few minutes the adjutant's voice called out: "First Battalion move on to the southern edge of the wood."

"Get up, lads! Form up on the road by sections!"

The road was a shambles; an overturned limber with broken wheels, a gun rolled over on its side in the ditch, helmets, rifles, pools of blood, cries and moans from the wounded and dying. We moved on in line of companies to the wood that still lay under artillery fire. Müssig-brodt appeared with Alfred – thank goodness both unhurt – and I got into the saddle. On the road, more horses, sometimes two or three in a heap still yoked together, dead or in the agonies of death; more men in most gruesome attitudes, shot or run over in the stampede, with here and there a machine gun lying among them. On, on, over it all! How splendid the steadiness of my men despite their yellow-green faces!

At the southern edge of the wood we halted by a group of houses. In front of us, a broad, open plateau to all appearances wallowing in peace and sunshine, but at the southern end of it guns boomed and a veil of whitish smoke hung about a line of poplars on the distant horizon; the enemy's artillery position. From there the shells hummed and hurtled towards us, bursting, not over the wood now, but away in front where the skirmishing lines of the Fusiliers were advancing. In front, behind, and in the midst of them fountains of black smoke and dust spurted up out of the ground; and one, two, or three grey figures collapsed on to the field.

Beyond the group of houses was the battalion staff, standing behind a shed. Lieutenant von Steuben, the adjutant, waved. Was it to me? Yes – gee up, Alfred. The major pointed to the right with outstretched arm: "Bloem, will you deploy your company on the right of the Fusilier line for an enveloping attack on the right corner of Sancy village? Don't go beyond the southern end of the village!" And in an undertone he added: "It will be a nasty job – God help you …" As if to confirm these parting words a dozen black fountains of smoke and earth spurted up in a line along the very part of the field we were to cross, and a few seconds later another dozen. So I was to take my company through that?

My nerves seemed to brace themselves up for the great test. At last the hour had struck; so be it. I saluted, turned Alfred about and trotted back to my company: "B Company is to attack, lads! It's a raging hell in front, but we've got to go through it. I rely on you all." Dismounting, I gave the order: "B Company extend to the right – double!" My "staff" came out to me and together we moved out in front of the company, the whole line emerging from the group of houses in excellent order and past the battalion commander, who saluted his "*morituri*."

In front of us, now scarcely a hundred yards off, a long line of little puffs of white cloud floated in the air, and below them a small forest of black fountains of smoke and dirt. Death, I'm ready for you! Here is my forehead, here is my heart! Strike, if you wish! And as I went into it, a shout of triumph, a wild, unearthly singing surged within me, uplifting and inspiring me, filling all my senses. I had overcome fear; I had conquered my mortal bodily self. And I glanced back on my little army; they were following, a long line of high-held foreheads, of strong, gallant hearts. Bless you, children – my children!

Nearer and nearer the barrage, to the messengers of death. Welcome! Welcome! Strange, though, that of a sudden no more shells were coming. All was quiet in front of us. No treacherous white lambs frolicking in the sky, no explosions, no miniature volcanoes; the black smoke and cloud of dust was gradually clearing away in front. Just a pause in the fight, no doubt; any moment the storm would break again and burst over us with redoubled fury. We were already crossing the zone where for half an hour volley after volley of shells had ploughed up the field, bits of shell, empty shells, dud shells – shrapnel that had not burst – lying all about, with every here and there a mutilated Fusilier among them.

On, on, to the village edge! Now our own guns were coming into action, howitzer-batteries, and their high-explosive shells passed over us and crashed into the roofs of the village, rusty-red clouds of smoke and debris towered up into the sky. The church spire cracked like a bit of timber, and toppled on one side. On, on!

Strange, though, still no enemy shells. Where were they? Had they gone, cleared out? Was it possible? And as I marched on, sweating, across the torn-up acres and saw Death retreating away from us, the nervous reaction that overcame me was so intense that I suddenly laughed, laughed outright at the way I had braced myself up to such a high pitch of heroism!

Behind me, too, I heard talking and giggling, and looking round saw my staff grinning, and then they too burst out laughing. Turning my head still further I saw the whole line of B Company were laughing, the corners of their mouths almost reaching their ears. We all felt the same. Who would have imagined how amazingly comic it is having worked oneself up with heaven-inspired ardour to meet Death like a true hero, for her not to come to the trysting-place? No doubt about it now, she had definitely gone, away over the far horizon. I almost wept with joy and laughter.

We halted on the ridge at the southern edge of the village, according to orders. The Fusiliers, on our left, were in the village itself. We lay down, literally convulsed at the relief of it all. After half an hour an order came that the regiment was to billet in the village, battalions to move in to their quarters. We marched in and piled arms in the main street. While waiting for the allotment of billets the haggard face of a civilian appeared in a cellar window. I told him to come out. He shuffled out, trembling from head to foot. "I'm a refugee, sir, a poor, starved refugee – don't kill me, sir, don't kill me …"

"I haven't the slightest intention of doing so. Where are you from?"

"Oh, sir! I've come a long way, from the north, from the Ardennes … we've been on the road three weeks – three weeks, and nothing to eat – "

"We – who's we?"

"There's me, sir, and the mother and my wife and the babies, sir, the poor little babies … " Looking down I could see eyes staring through the cellar window out of two frightened, sorrowful little faces …

"Any bread, lads! Give some to these miserable, starving kids." They had some left – the last crumbs of the seventy-five loaves from the baker's cellar in Taillefontaine. The little mites emerged, stretched out filthy, dirty little paws, and set-to like hungry dogs on all the crumbs they could get.

"Oh, sir! How kind you are – may my mother come out – and my wife?"

"We do not eat women, any more than we eat children." A dishevelled, withered old woman and a young wife appeared, their travel-stained clothes hanging slovenly about them.

"Now, tell me, madame, why were you so foolish as to run away from us?"

"Oh, sir, it was the papers – those wretched papers. If you only knew all the things they have written in them about you. You beat men to death, you burn the children, you violate the women – yes, sir, all that and more has been printed in the papers about you!"

"Lads, you must listen to this – and hear what a pack of scalliwags you are!" and, for the edification of my Grenadiers, I translated the information to them word for word. They listened in silence, angrily. "I'd like to have the throat of the man who wrote that between my fingers … " growled Sauermann. Before very long the babies were having a ride on the knees of the Huns and pulling at their long, dusty beards.

At last we moved into our billets. A big farmhouse with its yard and buildings took the whole of the 1st Battalion. All the officers had rooms; the battalion commander and the two captains even had beds: it seemed rather frivolous to undress within range of the enemy's guns, but one's weary bones needed all the rest they could get. Tables were set out in the farmyard, and how delicious it was to breathe the cool air of the perfect summer night after the blazing, suffocating heat of the day. While the officers of the battalion, all that were left, were sitting together enjoying a reunion, a great massacre of hens was taking place around us, and Elberling and Liebsch were thoroughly happy slaughtering the finest bullock on the premises. All of a sudden there was a shout and scurry throughout the yard; and from out a doorway marched the bullock, his massive head lowered and his eyes full of sullen anger. A number of hands tried to catch hold of his horns, to turn him round again into his stall, but he tossed his head to right and left, and to right and left men fell to the ground. They let him alone after that, and he strode on unopposed through the crowd of brave warriors out of the yard into the open field and joined a lot of cows. We went on with our dinner, while the youngsters went on with their merry work all round us. The fine-flavoured Burgundy from the farm cellar sparkled in the bright light of a full moon; and did any of us think for a moment of the dead, of the death-drive of those gunners in the sunken road, of the Fusiliers shelled to pieces in that ploughed-up field? But the soldier mustn't think, mustn't remember, otherwise he couldn't stand it.

Had we known the situation and what lay in front of us, the Burgundy mightn't have tasted quite as excellent as it did.

Chapter Fourteen

The Fight Continues

As I write I know something, though far from all, of what was happening about us and around us at this period; but at the time itself we just swam, as it were, in mid-stream of the flood of events in blissful ignorance, except, perhaps, for those occasional uncanny feelings of general uneasiness, for no especial reason other than such as losing touch with Bülow's Second Army, or the apparently complete absence of communications behind, or the news gradually trickling through to us that our artillery were running short of ammunition. The most depressing factor of all, however, was our own exhausted selves: we were all literally done in. For exactly two weeks, since August 23rd, we had been in constant touch with the enemy, and lately had had minor encounters with him daily: If this was modern warfare we had not been trained, nor were we prepared for it. A year later, in the Russian offensive, I survived without difficulty, mental and physical hardships incomparably greater, but my standards by then had completely altered. At this early period, however, our ideas of war, and mine especially, owing to my work on the war novels, were based entirely on the 1870 campaign. A battle, according to that, would begin at 6 am and end, victoriously of course, at 6 pm, then a hymn of thanksgiving, "Now thank we all our God," and bivouac on the battlefield: early the next morning the pursuit would begin and be continued for two enjoyable weeks with two rest-days in comfortable billets, followed by another good, healthy battle in the grand manner.

But this was something entirely different, something utterly unexpected. For a month now we had been in the enemy's country, and during that time had been on the march incessantly, from about Neuss to south-east of Paris, without a single rest-day. We were astonished at our own powers of endurance. How many miles had I covered the last few days on foot, being so tired that if I got on my horse I fell asleep at once and would have fallen off? How many anxious discussions had I had with Ahlert regarding the company's boots: scarcely a single pair that hadn't a nail sticking through the soles, which were as thin as paper. A few more days on the road and my Grenadiers would be marching barefoot.

At breakfast the next morning came a curious order that further depressed our sorely tried spirits: "The regiment will assemble at 7 am in the hollow north of Sancy, facing north." North! Backwards, in fact! Most strange. "During the march we shall return through places already passed through, and the men are therefore to be told that the future movements of the corps are in no way to be regarded as a retreat. Having thrown back the enemy that was opposing it from the south, the First Army is now to advance against the east front of Paris to guard against hostile operations from that place." Very odd, indeed. We had missed the triumphal entry into Paris, but that didn't matter: these remarkable explanations as to the future were unconvincing, however, and in spite of them we all felt definite anxiety when the regiment assembled.

As we waited, lying on the grass for the order to move off, a band suddenly struck up. What on earth was that for? It was the band of the Fusilier battalion. Their dead of yesterday's attack were being buried: their colonel was standing bareheaded, and at the head of the graves the band was playing a funeral hymn. Our thoughts were sufficiently gloomy as it was, and the addition of these lamentations at such a moment was enough to break our miserable hearts. A terrible homesickness overcame me; my trembling hands felt in my pocket for the photographs of my loved ones, but hot tears so clouded my eyes that I could scarcely distinguish their features. I felt ashamed to face my men; but looking round I saw that most of them, lying there in the damp grass, had their faces buried in their arms, and many were sobbing. One single overpowering desire for rest, peace, and home had unnerved all this gallant host of warriors, the 12th Grenadiers.

The march began, and within half an hour we were back again at the scene of the stampede in the sunken road. Engineers were digging graves; and the dead, ashy pale and distorted, had been laid out in rows by the roadside: the bellies of the dead horses were swelling with the increasing heat of the sun. Instead of going on the way we had come, through Pierrelez, we turned off to the left, westwards, towards Paris in fact. There was a sigh of relief. If we really were starting a retreat …! and yet it still seemed something of the kind, for behind us the rumbling noise of a battle was breaking out afresh. Today, for once anyhow, we were not next to the enemy, the Brandenburg Guard Regiment being behind us: it would be their turn to do something.

All of a sudden: "Halt … pile arms!" What was to happen now? The artillery passed on through us, and then – then came the Brandenburg Guard Regiment! They marched on past, too. So now we were again left next to the enemy. They had scarcely got by when an order came: "The regiment will turn about and march back to Sancy!"

Good God! Sancy … back to that damned Sancy again! However, no matter. Orders are orders! Set your teeth, lads, and back we go! On the way a rumour came along with good authority that the whole III Corps had been taken from the First Army and placed at the disposal of Bülow's Second Army, and that it was to remain at Sancy ready to support if required. Within half an hour we were marching for the third time through the avenue of bloated horses. They were beginning to smell now, revoltingly, and I was retching, almost sick, before we were past.

We were to take up a position in the same old hollow north of Sancy, but before arriving there a message came: "52nd Regiment is in action south of Sancy and needs support immediately." We deployed and advanced west of the village towards another called, if my motor map didn't lie, Angers. What were we to do now? Occasional shrapnel were bursting near us, but no rifle or machine-gun fire, and the village appeared unoccupied. Were we to take it? No. A message from the battalion: "Do not go beyond the ridge." So we halted on the ridge: all the same, I would find out if anyone was in the village. "Boettcher, you're a fine strong fellow; take four sturdy lads from your section, and see if that village in front has any enemy in it; and mind you all come back, understand?"

So this was another battlefield, a peaceful summer landscape, glistening in the sun and apparently completely deserted, except for ourselves and on our left a company of the 52nd, which, like us, was lying extended out in the open field without any cover. The enemy's artillery-fire now increased, but the shrapnel were bursting at random over a large area. The enemy evidently didn't see us yet, and we certainly couldn't see him. The patrol returned: "No enemy in the village." Well done, Boettcher.

The shrapnel now seemed to burst close to us more consistently, some a hundred, then fifty, then only ten yards in front, smothering us with a cloud of dust and dirt, and we experienced for the first time the awful sensation of lying in the open under artillery-fire unable to reply: no order to dig in, and in those days nothing was done without an order. Soon the air was rent with the screams and bursts of shell, in front, behind, and all about us. My men, lined out to right and left of me, lay pale to their very lips. With no enemy to fire at, some had pulled their packs over their heads as cover, others had buried their heads in corn-stooks, following the policy of the ostrich. Someone running crouching from behind plumped down beside me: it was a young artillery subaltern, Baron von Freytag-Loringhoven, son of a former and much-respected commander of my regiment.

"May I ask you a question, sir?"

"By all means, a dozen if you like!"

"My battery commander wishes to know if you have seen the position of any of the enemy's guns?"

"Not one, tell him. A more harmless, peaceful-looking bit of country I've seldom seen." He scanned the horizon with his glasses. "You're right, sir. There's no sign of them. They must be behind the ridge, beyond that road, and firing indirect. If so, they must have an observer in front somewhere. Are there any enemy in that village, sir?"

"The village is empty. My patrol has just reported that there's not a soul in it."

"The church-tower, is that empty too?"

"That I couldn't say. Boettcher, did you go up the church-tower?" – "No, sir."

"Good; I think that's it then. We'll try and put the observer out of action, anyhow," and full of youthful content the slim figure thanked me and crept away.

A few minutes later an order from the battalion: "B Company will retire to the road and occupy the embankment along it." Back again, why? What had we been lying here for in this open field with nothing to fire at, with no definite objective all this time? The order should have come three hours ago. Besides, how could I possibly go back and leave the company of the 52nd on my left without any support. "Pohlenz! Go across to the 52nd there, and tell the company commander that we've been ordered back to the road, and suggest that he does the same."

Pohlenz sloped off with his usual indifference along behind the extended line to the next company. At that moment from far away behind came something invisible and mysterious, yet colossal, hurtling at great speed towards us; it rent the air above our heads and passed away towards the village in front. Suddenly a yellow-green pillar of poisonous-looking smoke spurted up beyond the right of the church spire. Wschwschlwschlwschlwschl – another rushed past above us, this time just to the left of the spire, crash into a roof, and then another column of smoke. Evidently our heavy guns were ranging on the church with shrapnel. Then another, but making a different noise this time as it tore past overhead – God! what a noise too – a high-explosive shell this time crashed right into the spire. The whole spire and tower seemed to burst asunder, a great column of smoke shot up, and the beams of the belfry whirled through the air like a heap of black matchwood. When the smoke cleared the spire had gone – and anyone hiding in it, too. Almost simultaneously the enemy's artillery-fire ceased, as if automatically switched off. Goodbye, Mr Observer.

Pohlenz returned. "Well, what did the captain say?"

He said we could do whatever we liked; that he's all right where he is, and intends to stay there." Damn it, a nice friendly sort of message! "Niestrawski, run along back to battalion headquarters, and say that a company of the 52nd lying next us has had no order to retire, and ask if I am to leave it in front here alone."

For a quarter of an hour all was quiet; the enemy were probably organising another observation-post, for then the shells began to come once more, a regular hail of them, as if to make up for lost time and to give their revenge, screaming and crashing like mad things all about us and black fountains spurting up all over the field. We realised now for the first time, however, that a bombardment of this kind, though nerve-shattering, has little effect in comparison with the quantity of ammunition used, only one of my company being killed and three wounded by it – one terribly smashed about, his piercing cries sounding high and shrill above the fury of the concert.

Niestrawski came back, apparently a charmed life too, though his bearded face was at least two shades paler than Pohlenz's gutter-snipe physiognomy. His message was that we were to retire, irrespective of the 52nd. To satisfy my conscience I sent once more to the captain of the next company that I had definite orders from my battalion to retire and was about to go back. To make the message more impressive I told Sergeant Döring to take it, and to ask the captain to retire in conjunction with us.

In a few minutes Döring returned. "Well, what did he say this time?"

"He threw things at me ... "

"Oh, well, we'll leave him, then, and let him die in his last ditch."

To avoid attracting the enemy's notice I ordered the men to go back one at a time, starting from both flanks. But none moved. I understood. None of them wished to be the first to turn their backs on the enemy so long as their friends stayed on in front. So I had to tell section commanders to order each man back by name. I and Döring went back with the last ten widely extended. The wounded were carried back to the road and placed under a culvert for shelter.

The whole battalion was digging in along the roadside. "Get out your entrenching tools, lads, and dig for your lives." Our own artillery fire had stopped altogether, whether on purpose or through lack of ammunition we didn't know, but we were being left entirely to the mercy of the enemy's guns. Their shells roared and howled above us like a hurricane blowing. The low embankment by the roadside gave scanty protection, and the stony soil was difficult to dig with the light spade-end of the entrenching tools. The one soothing remedy in such a situation was tobacco, but, unfortunately, we had none left. Previously whenever under fire I had lit up a cigar; but now, when most needed, this great comfort was not available, neither were cigars falling out of the enemy's shrapnel.

During these hours of patient endurance all kinds of thoughts passed through one's mind, and not at all the sort that the uninitiated might imagine. One did not think of dying; all the events of one's life did not process past one's eyes, one did not think of wife and children, nor of home and country, nor of King, nor God, nor fame, nor immortality – nothing like that at all, but quite ordinary, everyday thoughts. One wondered whether the cookers would be able to get up when it got dark, how much longer the blackguards would go on firing at us, what they thought they were gaining by such idiotic waste of ammunition, the silly fools! – crash, a shrapnel burst above me, one of its bullets knocked my left heel. I thought my foot must be in bits – no, only the spur bent – the bullet lay there by my foot, three-quarters of an inch in diameter. Wapp! A "dud" shell, falling smack on the ground without bursting. Wapp! another dud. Did our artillery still exist? A shabby trick to leave us in the lurch like this. If I was wounded, how should I get to a dressing-station? I'd have to stay here till the blackguards had finished. Rossberg, with a running conversation full of wit, kept up the men's spirits: a splendid fellow, I must recommend him for a decoration. Would Willy Weise remember to bring up my overcoat with him tonight? The dew was beginning to fall already. It was getting dusk. Wapp! another dud – only a couple of yards from us. If that had been a live shell! My men's faces were rigid, pale, their eyes almost bursting from their sockets, the whites quite red, the lids swollen and all riveted on me, watching my expression, my movements. At that moment I learnt the meaning of the word "leader," what an obligation it carried and how, too, it increased one's power of self-control and mental strength beyond measure. "Don't let your eyes drop out, children; it might be much worse." At last, at long last, darkness crept on to our rescue. One last frenzied salvo full of hate and fury, then the enemy's guns suddenly ceased; all was still, silent, at peace again.

No sooner had we begun to move about in the open again than two orders reached us: "Battalions will make preparation to hold their present position against strong enemy attacks tonight"; and the other: "Listening patrols will be sent out in front and take with them matches and bundles of straw: as soon as the enemy's advance is definitely seen they will set fire to the straw and clear the front: that will be the signal to open fire."

"Got that, lads! Get on with your digging then!" It was a warm night, and we were all soon sweating. I, too, got hold of a spade and began to dig like a nigger, glad to feel the blood throbbing through my veins and my cramped limbs coming to life again. A silvery mist rose from the wide expanse of grassland about us, but so thin that the light of the full moon easily penetrated it. It was hot work; and the men, one after another, began to take off their coats, exposing to my astonished sight naked arms and low-cut necks frilled all round with most dainty lace; in fact, ladies' underwear. The explanation was simple: it was the best substitute Ahlert had been able to pick upon his foraging expeditions to replace the men's shirts, which had become so matted with sweat that they were no longer wearable.

Once again I slept in a trench, squeezed like a sardine between Sauermann and Niestrawski, Pohlenz curled up at our feet, the fag-end of a cigarette between his lips as always. Did ever a king sleep better guarded?

I was roused in the middle of the night. An order from regimental headquarters: "Send out an officer's patrol southwards to find where the enemy are." Below the message the battalion commander had written: "Patrol will be sent out by B Company."

"Tell Lieutenant Chorus to come here." Within a few minutes the gallant fellow, in normal life an official in the Prussian law-courts, was walking away with eight men into the mist, into the unknown. Two hours later he was back, woke me, and reported: "I got to the main road from Villiers-St Georges to Provins and stayed close to it unnoticed; columns of the enemy were marching along it south-westwards in disorder." "You've done well, Chorus. Bravo! Write that down, and we'll send it along to headquarters."

Neither Chorus nor I guessed at that moment that he and his patrol had penetrated farther into France than any other German soldier.

Chapter Fifteen

La-Ferté-sous-Jouarre

Regimental order: "The enemy has retired towards Paris. The advance against the east front of the capital will be resumed as ordered yesterday."

That sounded all right. At the first streak of dawn we were on the move again. It was just getting light when we marched for the fourth time through the avenue of dead horses, their bellies now swollen up like big balloons, and the stench perfectly awful. My empty stomach revolted. I was almost sick, but fortunately I remembered I had some chocolate in my pocket and stuffed my mouth with it, and so passed through. There followed another endless, most grim day of marching, needing all that was left of my men's nerves and legs to endure it. We marched through La Ferté-Gaucher and back across the Grand Morin, then up a hill and halted ... in Grand-Doucy, in the very same orchard we had had our midday rest three days ago – only three days! And again a promised halt of two hours was interrupted after half an hour by another order: "The march will be continued with all speed, regardless of the comfort of the troops." No reason for this frantic haste was given. Most strange.

From Grand-Doucy we descended into the valley of the Petit Morin to Sablonnières back along the same road we had come three days before. In the village the Fusiliers had stormed our wounded were still lying, some in a chapel close to the road. Alarmed and bewildered they watched us go past: we were unable to take them with us, and all eventually fell into the enemy's hands.

We crossed the Petit Morin and thence turned off north-westwards by a road we had not been on before. The sun blazed down on us, the heat intensely oppressive, and perhaps even more oppressive the thought of a terrible, hideous possibility. Forwards, forwards, was the order; but weren't we actually going just a little backwards!

The sun was lowering in the west. In the far distance the boom of artillery fire without intermission: a battle was going on somewhere. Where, though? No – impossible! But it was unmistakable, undeniable – it was to north of us. To the north – whence we had marched days ago, and whither we were now marching – a battle was being fought. The realisation of all that this meant was enough to stagger the most courageous heart. By midday the condition of the men was such that we company commanders rode up to the major and told him a halt was imperative, otherwise half our companies would collapse on the road. Shortly afterwards the whole regiment, or rather the two-thirds of it that were left, halted in a field, where we all lay prostrate: no jokes, no complaints, but just a bitter indifference.

On again! The sun had set long since, and we marched on into the night. Where were we? Someone said we were near Meaux, and Meaux I knew was twenty-five miles from Paris. In that case we were still advancing if anything. We entered a dense forest: occasionally between the tops of the trees was a strip of blue-black brocade, silver-spangled, but otherwise it was pitch-dark within, black as ravens' feathers. It was hopeless to try and keep in column of fours, one could see nothing, but imagined the company must be in complete chaos. And yet not a voice to be heard, not a laugh, not even a curse: a leaden silence, just the steady monotonous tramp – tramp – tramp of many hundred aching, dead-tired feet.

And so it went on for apparently hours. Whoever was asking his troops to do what we were doing must have been in desperate straits, staking his all on it; for it was almost a superhuman demand. We became just a flock of helpless sheep pattering along in the dark. What did it matter? What did anything matter? We were losing spirit; it was too much.

At last the forest came to an end, and we emerged into open country. A little further on through the night mist were lights, dim little lights dotted about over a fair-sized area. Evidently a town: Meaux, no doubt. I thought of that cry that struck terror into the hearts of the Parisians in 1870, a few days after Sedan: "The Prussian Lancers are in Meaux!" And now, well, now we, the Brandenburg Grenadiers, were in Meaux!

As we came to the first houses, the feeble lamp-light from a window showed up on the wall opposite the usual blue-painted signboard with the name of the village in white letters. I flashed my electric-torch on it and read "La Ferté-sous-Jouarre …"

So it wasn't Meaux after all, and a glance at my motor-map showed that we were nowhere near it: thirteen miles further up the Marne, in fact, and further away from Paris. The streets were deserted and in darkness except for an occasional dim light from a window. No sign of a halt: we turned to the left, out of the town, and began to climb a steep hill. That hill was the last straw! One after another men reeled and staggered out of the column and collapsed into the ditch. By the time we reached the top only a tottering horde of shadowy forms, in no order or formation, remained of the battalion. At last, like everything else, the march came to an end, and this time in a hill-top village, apparently empty, and in utter darkness except for the ghostly light of a pale moon.

"I will allot the houses!" shouted the voice of the battalion commander. "These four to B Company … "

"Right! Good night, major."

"Good night, Bloem. It will be a short one, though. Midnight now, and we move off again at 4 am."

My own lodging was passable, and still inhabited by an elderly couple, trembling yet friendly-disposed, who prepared us a meal of boiled eggs and potatoes with coffee and wine. Even a bed was put at my disposal; but before enjoying it, though dead-beat, my conscience would not let me rest till I had gone through the rooms in the adjoining houses to see if my poor wretched lads were settling in all right. For eight days these houses, evacuated by their owners, had been used as billets by friend and foe. I thought I had by now experienced most of the horrors of war, but here was something I had not yet seen: I mean what eight days and nights of war-conditions can do to ordinary human dwellings, without any fighting or shells or wounded in their vicinity. By the light of the flickering candles the men had with them I saw in every room nothing but a mess of filth and muck, as if a horde of lunatics had satisfied all their mad desires in them. As for the smell, well, I was as nearly sick as when among the dead horses that morning. So this was the stench of war – healthy, wholesome, purifying war!

Thoroughly disgusted, I returned to my bed with its white sheets, in itself remarkable evidence of what I had already noticed, namely, that both friend and foe treated with utmost respect all those houses whose owners had remained in them. Barely three hours' rest when my pocket alarm-clock woke me, the luminous hands pointing to 3 am. I dressed, for on mornings such as this if the company commander is not the first on parade nothing gets done.

Ahlert reported the company all present; those who had fallen by the wayside the night before had all joined up again. Somehow, every one of them had found his way "home," as no doubt they too had begun to realise that to stay behind now meant falling into the enemy's hands. While dressing I had left behind my identity disc, and, mentioning it to some men near me, I noticed a strange look of fear pass across their faces: an old superstition among soldiers which, however, didn't come true in my case.

Chapter Sixteen

Withdrawal Over The Marne

It was still dark as we marched back from our hill-top village, Jouarre, down again into the town of La Ferté in the Marne valley. In the dawn light the place looked quite changed; the streets were now filled with a host of men, moving back across the Marne, a whole army, and an army retreating. It must have been obvious now to the most dense what was happening. We knew well what a victorious advance was like and the spirit that animated it; we had lived with it for a month; but this was very different. We did not understand, but we could see, and that sufficed. The town reflected this fateful hour in its country's struggle for existence. Snuggling so pleasantly under a gentle slope of the Marne uplands it must have been a most charming place in peace-time, but now ... The houses were deserted and shuttered up, their doors smashed open by a succession of troops searching for a lodging; those on both banks of the river had had great holes torn in their walls and all the windows broken by the force of the explosions when the bridges were blown up, the curtains inside were hanging in shreds, and the furniture all smashed to pieces. The few inhabitants left skulked about like shadows, like poverty-stricken beggars.

I was so impressed by the sight that, when we halted just after crossing back over the Marne, I made my company a short speech: "You see that, men," I said, pointing back at the town, "that's what they hoped to do to us, and now we've done it to them. You can understand now why we are here: so that that should take place in this foreign land and not in our own homes. That is why we have had not a minute's rest for the past four weeks, that is why you have marched the soles off your feet, that is why we have fought in a dozen engagements, and it is for that, too, so many of our friends have given their lives. Think that over, men, and be proud and thankful that it is you, you yourselves, who have spared your homes such a fate!"

At last the jumble of men, horses, guns, and vehicles massed in front and behind us unravelled itself, and the column marched on up the hill. We were hardly out of the town before staff-officers from another corps galloped past covered in dust. Their news soon leaked through to us company commanders: east of the Ourcq a battle had been raging for the past two days. The enemy, based on Paris and with superior numbers, had made a desperate attack against the IV Reserve Corps, our right-flank guard: the II and IV Corps had already hurried to its assistance, and now, today, the III and IX Corps were also to join in the battle. The enemy had a great superiority in artillery as the battle zone was within range of the Paris forts. For this reason every available gun was to be pushed on without delay and the roads left clear for them; the infantry keeping to the fields by the roadside. They, too, were to march to the battle with all speed, otherwise there was a danger of our resistance breaking down.

This report was confirmed by the rumbling thunder of battle that was getting louder and louder ahead of us. Forwards, then! On, on into it! Once again the tired-out bones, aching feet, and worn-out boots had to give all that was left of them.

The Fusiliers, in front, had already crossed the top of the hill that separated us from the Ourcq valley, and one of them, Captain von Freyhold, rode back to me, the leading company: "Look out, Bloem, when you get to the top! You'll see something!" I trotted on, filled with suspense, and I saw …

In the foreground was a deep valley, the further slope rising up to a rolling plateau covered with small woods and villages. At the back was a long ridge of hills that stood up like the wall of a gigantic fortress, and along the whole length of this horizon lay a thick, motionless layer of mist several miles in length. Sudden flashes, like lightning, and columns of white smoke continually shot up through and above it. "Some artillery position, eh?" said Freyhold, who had come with me.

I can remember as if it was yesterday how at that moment our real situation was suddenly revealed to me. Up till then our only actual experiences had been those of a successful walk-over, a far stiffer one than in 1870, although the fights of the latter had been more impressive. Nevertheless, with the exception of that night at Tertre, the idea of a retreat, a defeat, or the possibility of a disastrous ending to the war, had never seriously entered our minds. We had always had superiority of numbers in every fight; but now, over there, was something quite fresh, a new experience and a terrible one: a superior opponent. This sudden complete turn of the wheel of fate gave me my first glimmering of what war, and this one in particular, really signified, and the full extent of the danger that lay ahead, not to the life of the individual but to the greatness and the very life itself of the German nation. And, while I watched, a sudden and complete transformation took place within me. Till now I had been an individual entity, fighting, suffering, worrying, hoping: at this moment that individual self ceased to exist, was sacrificed on the altar of patriotism, and from its dead ashes it was resurrected as one small piece of living, struggling, wounded Germany. Some mental process of the same kind must have taken place within us all at this time, for the officers rode on silently as if the power of speech had left them, and the men's faces had a changed expression, that look of callous indifference had become one of obdurate determination.

Our artillery began to arrive, rattling and clattering past us. First the light field-guns and then the heavies, their great horses pounding on streaming with sweat, their muscles standing out like cords of steel. And we continued our march alongside in silence, hurrying to the battle, down into the valley of the Ourcq, and through the town of Lizy. A crowd of wounded and prisoners – prisoners too, thank God – streamed past without end. We were now close to the battlefield, the noise of it drowning all other sound, and began to ascend the further slope of the valley. Here we deployed and halted, awaiting the final order for the advance.

But the order to attack did not come. We were moved about, first to the west, then back slightly to the north, until finally we stopped again on a hill south-west of Le-Plessis-Placy, just out of range of the enemy's artillery. About a thousand yards ahead we watched the shrapnel bursting and the high explosives tearing up the ground. The arrival of our guns, the heavies especially, appeared to have relieved the situation, so much so that the cookers were brought up and gave us a meal, though we expected every moment to have the enemy's shells on top of us.

To our right, nearby, was an ancient weather-beaten church surrounded by a walled-in cemetery. I went across through the cemetery into the building. A glaring light shone through the windows in the rough stone-wall above the altar, and fell direct on a large, quaint plaster-figure of the resurrected Christ giving the Blessing and standing on a mass of cloud, all in white. Beneath, lying all over the floor of the building on a carpet of straw, were at least a hundred severely wounded, some in delirium, some with the death-rattle in their throats, some crying, but most of them silent. I fled from the place and went on to an equally ancient and completely deserted farm, deciding to stake my claim to it in case we should have to spend the night where we were. In any case it would be shelter from a heavy storm that was blowing up and would give cover against shrapnel if necessary. I went back and brought my company along to it. The only disturbing factor was a ghastly smell coming from the yard, that had evidently been used for some days past as a slaughter-house, a dozen bullocks' heads, entrails and hides lying about putrefying. Shovelling the pestilential remains into wheelbarrows, we emptied them into a disused chalk-pit near by. Very soon the men had settled down in the rooms and sheds, and we officers sat in an unspeakably filthy room on a pile of broken bedsteads. Outside a downpour of rain came on, and the thunder of guns continued without cessation. As soon as the rain stopped I gladly left our room of foul smells for the open air, and met an unknown staff-officer at the door.

"What regiment is this, please?"

"12th Grenadiers"

"That's III Corps, isn't it? Good; then where's your commanding officer?" I directed him.

After a few minutes came the order to move, and the regiment marched away southwards. It was getting dusk, and our attention was held by a village on some high ground in front being very heavily shelled. The noise and the effect of the explosions was greater than any we had yet seen: the guns of the Paris forts, some said, while others suggested English naval guns.[1] We halted east of the village, named Trocy, and between us was a deep hollow which the enemy was shelling as thoroughly as the wretched Trocy, now for the most part in flames. Shell after shell crashed into it, sending up clouds of smoke and debris, the most gigantic and terrifying we had experienced. We gazed spellbound at the spectacle.

It appeared that throughout the day some of our heavy batteries had been in position in the hollow, and had been discovered by an enemy aeroplane observer. Half an hour later they had been so smashed about that only a few odd guns had been saved.

As darkness drew on the roar of battle suddenly ceased, after a final mad burst of firing, a usual custom apparently, and soon afterwards we were ordered forward to relieve the remnants of the 44th Reserve Brigade, the 32nd and 82nd Regiments, in the front line. We marched on across the hollow, then up the hill into the village, which was now gradually crumbling away and burning into a heap of rubble. Dead men lay in the road, shadowy forms passed by our equally shadowy forms, voices asked "What regiment? Where are you going?" A captain, wandering

1   Guns of the French Sixth Army (General Manoury) that was advancing against the right wing of the German battle-front on the Ourcq.

aimlessly and alone, spoke to me: his speech was confused, and the light of my torch showed a haggard face with the restless shifting eyes of a madman: "I once had a company. I'm all that's left of it." On all sides was the tramping of troops, the clatter of horses, the rattle of guns on the march, and the shouting or moaning of human beings. "Where is the staff of the 44th Reserve Brigade?" "A Company, where's A Company?" "Stretcher-bearers wanted! Stretcher-bearers!" "Friends, do give us a hand; don't let me lie here, I'm dying." And all in pitch darkness, no moon, no stars, and the flames from the burning houses had died down to a smouldering glow.

Someone asked for the commander of the 1st Battalion, and reported himself to the major as a guide. The companies were split up: "A Company will go to the right to the brick quarry, the other three companies under Captain Bloem will follow the guide to the trenches of the 32nd Regiment and relieve them." Müssigbrodt took my horse, and I went on foot with the guide, followed by the companies, to the trenches on the far side of the village, and reported to the commander there. He said he had no orders to be relieved, and so would stay where he was till he had. I halted the companies and went back myself to the major, who told me to make another trench a hundred yards behind the existing one, and stay in it so long as the 32nd Regiment remained. I returned, took the companies to the line ordered, and they began to dig. No prospect of any more to eat or drink that night, that couldn't be helped; but more maddening still was the fact that we were told nothing of what was happening, of how the battle was going, nor of what was expected of us on the morrow. Nevertheless, the men made no word of complaint, no sign of discontent. "Dig, lads, dig; the sooner you've finished the longer you can sleep."

Exhausted and fed up, I slept soundly for two hours pressed close between my "staff" in a damp, stony trench. The expected enemy attack never materialised. I was wakened before it was light by an orderly: "The battalion will assemble in the hollow east of Trocy."

In that hollow! Let's only hope we shan't stay in it long ... Later the major told me we were to remain in it in support of the 44th Reserve Brigade. "Impossible, major!" I pointed out the mass of shell-craters. "They have the exact range of it." He agreed. "Come along then, Bloem, let's ride back into the village and find some better shelter." But every house and shed that still had any walls left was already occupied by troops. We passed "A" Company of our 2nd Battalion, and its popular commander, Lieutenant Hüffner, otherwise a professor at the university of Berlin-Wilmersdorf, who laughed a good morning at us, saying we had got up too late! He might well laugh, for he and his company were occupying one of the finest barns in the place.

We returned to the hollow, and column after column of the IV Reserve Corps tramped past us, going back! Many of the companies had obviously been reduced to sections. Some officers called out to us: "What do you think you're doing in that hollow?"

"We're ordered to stay here."

"You won't for long then. On the stroke of six the enemy's guns will start again, and you'll get it hot and strong if you stop there."

It was now ten minutes to six. The major rode up to Colonel von Reuter and got permission to move the battalion according to his own judgment. We marched

off at once out of the hollow to behind the village, and were hardly up the slope before the first shells burst behind us, sending up the same gigantic fountains of earth
and horrible sulphur-yellow smoke. "Lyddite," said some intelligent person. "They
were used in the Boer War, so they're English guns firing."

We found a very meagre shelter in a sunken track, and every couple of minutes
a hail of big iron cylinders as long as one's arm fell across the hollow to within fifty
yards of us, eventually making a curtain of foul smoke two hundred feet high. If the
enemy had spread his fire slightly eastwards, then good-bye 1st Battalion of the
12th Grenadiers. The men stared open-mouthed at this diabolical scene; and
when, during a short pause in the firing, the smoke curtain lifted a moment, we saw
that the heap of ruins once called Trocy village was being shelled too. So we were
thankful we hadn't gone there!

As we looked, a tremendous burst and the noise of crashing and splitting tim-
bers came from the village, and a dense yellow cloud of smoke enveloped the barn
where we had left Hüffner and his company. When the smoke dispersed, the barn
was no more, and his company were running away from the place in all directions.
Five minutes later a man came up without his helmet, his forehead covered in
blood; he was the sergeant-major of the unfortunate company. "My company commander is dead, sir The shell took away half his skull. Here is his watch and his
pocket-book."

"Thanks, sergeant, but you must give them to the adjutant of your battalion.
Had you any other losses?"

"Four more killed, sir, and I don't know yet how many wounded."

Every muscle was still quivering in the lean, tanned face of this gallant fellow.
One could see that he wanted to burst into tears, but he couldn't, so much horror
had stopped them, dried them up at their source. So farewell, my good Hüffner.
How often have you regaled your students with that line of Horace: "It is sweet and
decorous to die for one's country." Now you have done it – you know what it's like.
Farewell!

The fog of war was still thick about us; we did not know what was actually happening except for the fact that the enemy's offensive power seemed to have petered
out. The IV Reserve Corps had borne the brunt of it for the best part of three days,
and then the arrival of the other two corps had apparently sufficed to break it. We
had arrived too late on the scene to be of practical assistance. The troops that passed
through us had had a bad hammering, but they had done their job; the enemy's attack had failed.

So the order for us to attack, so long awaited, never came. From about midday
on we were moved from one place to another, orders, counter-orders, until finally
about 3 pm our fate was settled: "12th Grenadier Regiment will be taken from the
5th Infantry Division and come under the orders of the 22nd Reserve Division.
This latter division will retire through Vermelles to Fussy. Rearguard, 12th Grenadier Regiment."

In other words, we were to cover the retirement of the smashed-up 22nd Reserve Division. This was a retreat then, pure and simple. Not a shadow of doubt
about it now. Retreat!

We waited until the remainder of the 22nd Reserve had passed through, and
finally formed up ourselves and marched on behind them. Time and again a battal-

ion was deployed and waited facing the direction of the enemy, certain that if he was really the victor he would be hot in pursuit; but he never appeared, not a sign of him.

None of us could imagine what had happened. We were all too tired to try and fathom it, even to think about it. Orders were received and carried out almost automatically, then one dismounted and lay on the grass, mounting again when fresh orders arrived. One's mind, heart, and soul were consumed away; a great vast melancholy and misery hung over us all, seemingly over the whole world.

That was, for us, what is now called the Battle of the Marne.

Chapter Seventeen

The Retreat Continues

The enemy did not follow. Nevertheless, the fact remained that we ourselves were marching back, actually and undoubtedly retiring. With every step we took we were giving up a yard of the enemy's country we had conquered, more with our legs, perhaps, than with our rifles. It was a novel sensation; so novel, in fact, that one failed to grasp it, for we certainly had not been defeated, whole infantry divisions had as yet scarcely been engaged at all. The IX Corps, too, was, we heard, in the middle of a successful attack and about to roll up the whole French battle-line in front of us from its left flank when the order to retire reached it. Why? we were all asking – Why were we going back?

We retired into the Ourcq valley again, crossing the river north of Lizy. Here the valley widens out, forming a low-lying swampy area about four miles across and with no roads through it. We were astonished, therefore, to find that our engineers had constructed through this impassable district a track of logs and faggots wide enough to take two men abreast; the mounted arms having to make a wide circuit. As this must have taken quite two days to make, it pointed to the fact that our retreat had been thought out and arranged beforehand, and this belief put our minds more at rest. The march across this outlandish stretch of wooded marsh-land was strangely picturesque: aged peasants in patriarchal dress and half-savage children stared at us from queer log-huts here and there on the way. On a thickly wooded bit of dry ground we halted for our midday meal, though it was already getting dark, and filled our empty stomachs with the contents of the field-cooker. And then we went on into the night.

I have had countless night-marches since, but shall always remember this of the 9th – 10th September as the worst. When any two of us who took part in it meet nowadays, and one says to the other: "Do you remember that night-march?" he means this one, no matter how many others he has been in.

The ghostly procession became more and more silent as it got darker. A dense mist rose from the valley and covered the stars until it was pitch-black all around us; it was pitch-black within us, too. Up a hill out of the swamp, down another hill, then through woods, across ravines, over bleak uplands and through dead villages whose names we never knew, for no one had the energy to look at his map with an electric-torch. At last Lieutenant Faron, the adjutant of the regiment, rode back along the column calling out: "Two hours rest." We halted, the companies piled arms, and the men collapsed by the roadside where they stood, as if mown down. It was no easy job to get them up when the order came to fall in again; in fact, many could not be roused, twenty-nine of the regiment being reported as missing the next morning. Of the remaining hours of darkness of that terrible night I have scarcely the faintest shadow of memory. Müssigbrodt led my horse, and I stumbled along on foot, fast asleep. Incredible, but I did it.

The first streaks of dawn brought me back to consciousness, and we were marching through a very lovely valley. It turned out to be an upper reach of the Ourcq. In the distance was a peaceful-looking village, clean and well built. We entered it, Noroy-le-Bourg in white on a blue signboard, and halted, but it was 8.30 am before our quarters were allotted. A rumour ran round that we were to have a rest-day. What optimism! How childish to believe such a thing! And yet we did.

I was allotted a very smart little house: my bedroom had an enormous double bed and – clean sheets! Before getting between them a bath was essential, and as there was no bathroom I had a tin hip-bath brought to the room and took off my filthy clothes (we had not seen our baggage for fourteen days). My servant was about to pour the first bucket of water over me when I turned and suddenly caught sight of my body reflected in the full-length mirror of the wardrobe.

I nearly collapsed in astonishment. Lean as a skeleton, my skin covered with a regular crust of dust and sweat, my cheeks sunk in, my hair long and much greyer, my chin and jaw smothered with an untidy greyish beard: so that was me!

"Give me the soap, Grychta!" I would get that crust off anyhow, and how incredibly good it felt, a good lather and a wash down, again and again. And so to bed, to sleep for who knew how long? Just a glance first through the window into the garden: my grey company lying about all over it, and foraging in the orchard and among the vegetables. Ahlert saw me, and called up: "A grand cellar in the house, sir." "Splendid – give out a bottle of red wine for every two men, and pack the rest in the company wagon." And now, again, to bed.

I must have slept for about an hour and a half when I was wakened by a sound I had heard almost every day since Mons: that whining, snivelling, vomiting of the hounds of hell … Through the open window I could see up in the sky across the valley four little puffs of white cloud, that well-known flock of sheep back again. I jumped out of bed. "Grychta! Up you get!"

At that moment an orderly came to the door: "The battalion is to assemble on the road in five minutes, sir!" Good-bye, then, most attractive little room; good-bye, too, those fast-vanishing dreams of a rest-day. We had hardly formed up when another order came: "The southern edge of the village will be entrenched for defence." Orders, aggravating counter-orders, a rushing hither and thither and finally spades to work. We dug like coolies, and all the time the little white puffs of cloud were getting nearer and nearer.

The company had dug a trench about three feet deep alongside a garden hedge when another order arrived: "The regiment will form up and continue the march northwards." God damn it! All that sweat for nothing …

As soon as the last of the division we were covering had passed on, we followed, but halted again at Ancienville, where the battalion deployed off the road and took up a position. Our artillery fired like mad for a short time over our heads and then moved on. We followed suit, the march then taking us through woods, already showing the tints of autumn, down a steep valley and up on to high ground again. Another deployment. "Ahlert, did you pack in plenty of wine?"

"Ninety bottles, sir, and three bottles of champagne for the officers; all there was in the cellar!"

We were now back on our official maps and could see that the road the column was following descended shortly into another valley and across a stream at Corcy.

However, we waited extended out till 5 pm, but no enemy came. His shrapnel still seemed to be bursting over Noroy, or thereabouts, which we had left hours ago: he evidently thought we were still there. At last came the order to continue the retirement. My company was at the extreme end of the column, and Colonel von Reuter rode up to me: "Captain Bloem, I'm ordered by the 22nd Reserve Division to leave a company on this side of the valley until every man and straggler has crossed the bridge. As your company is the last you will have the honour of seeing this order carried out."

"I understand, colonel."

"Good luck, then." He shook my hand. I saluted, and he cantered away along the column. The other three companies of the battalion fell in, waved at us and marched on. My company stood by their line of piled rifles and looked at me. I looked at them, at the eighty-five men left out of the two hundred and fifty whom I had led from the barracks to Frankfort Station a month before, my heart so bursting with pride. They had heard the colonel's words. I could see they had understood. "Now, lads, I've got good news for you. We've brought along ninety bottles of claret on the company wagon. Sergeant Ahlert is bringing it back with the cooker, so we'll have a good meal. Then the enemy can come along and we'll be ready for him, won't we?"

"Yes, sir!" with one voice, and many a broad grin on the row of bearded faces. "And for us," I whispered, turning to Chorus and Schüler, "there are three bottles of champagne." They beamed.

Now for the outposts. "Corporal Wolff, will you take your section back about 300 yards along the road and put out a sentry-post. As soon as you see the enemy approaching in any numbers open a rapid fire – that will give us warning – and then fall back on us. I'll send your wine and food along to you." They went off and we settled down in comfort. Soon two enormous baskets full of red bottles were in the middle of the road being handed out, and in the ditch lay the three golden-necked bottles for us. The meal was accompanied by a babble of merriment. What did we care for danger! Old veterans now, so long as we had plenty of wine and food inside. The corks popped, and the cooker gave up its steaming contents.

Dusk stole on, the woods to our right all red and gold in the twilight. Behind them the booming of the enemy's guns: they were getting closer, the shells bursting beyond the wood almost level with us. Stragglers kept passing us along the road in ones and twos and groups, men of all arms of the service, most of them limping with worn-out feet or bleeding and bandaged.

"What are you waiting here for?" asked some. "The enemy may come any moment."

"What enemy?"

"Frenchmen, Englishmen, black men: all sorts. You'd better hurry up and come on."

Gradually this melancholy stream of remnants ceased, and the road was left deserted. Night came, and all was still once more. Cigars glowed red in the darkness, and silence lay over the contented company. Once again I had the feeling that I was living in a dream, that it was all a dream, some half-forgotten warrior epic of ages past. No enemy arrived, and, most strange of all, I had known from the first that he wouldn't. From the beginning I had not paid any serious attention to him, owing to an unshakable intuition within me that nothing was going to happen. We uncorked our last bottle of champagne. "To our loved ones at home!" and again we clinked glasses as the foam swirled up over their rims.

A cyclist rode up from behind. "Captain Bloem!"

"Here!" He jumped off.

"The major says the company is to march on again and join the battalion." In a few minutes the piquet was back and the company was moving away down the hill into the black night. We crossed the stream, where an NCO and four men of the engineers were waiting to blow up the bridge after us, and then on. No sign of the enemy; we were the last and yet not a vestige of him. What a miserable, sloppy kind of pursuit! If only it was the other way round, we'd give him a lesson and teach him how to do it! I rode on peacefully behind my company, the last company of the rearguard to one of the most battered German divisions in the battle: for two whole days the enemy had made no attempt to harass us. And I thought that if ever the French tried to make out that the battle on the Ourcq had been a victory …

And they have: so now I can give evidence that the legend of the victory of the Marne is an utter fraud. A German company whose duty it was to protect the hardest-hit division remained for four hours waiting for the pursuing enemy, and found nothing else to do than eat its fill and drain ninety bottles of claret. That was two days after the "Victory on the Marne," and the company was B Company of the 12th Grenadiers.

After a few hours we came up with the battalion which had had orders to entrench a position on the high ground nearby, north of Longpont. We took up our place in the line in pouring rain and complete darkness and dug a sort of trench. Wet and shivering, we were able to doze in it for a couple of hours, until about 4 am the order came to move again. There was a long halt on the road while the division in front was getting away. I looked at my Grenadiers in the dawn light, and scarcely recognised them. Covered in dirt and mud, their faces hidden behind tousled, untidy beards, their whole attitude showed utter exhaustion, and, worst of all, writ large on every bent head was the word "Retreat." Undefeated and yet going back. It is difficult to imagine without experience what that means, but it was enough to bring the bitterest tears to the dryest eyes.

As it got light we saw from our maps we were approaching the town of Soissons from the south west, and, in spite of all our worries, were still sufficiently credulous to imagine we should have a long rest in the town to buy things, soap, clean underclothing, and so on, even perhaps to have a real bath. Our march continued through a curiously formed valley, massive outcrops of rock towered up above the trees crowned by farmhouses built in a style of centuries past. I had to march on foot again for fear of falling asleep on the horse and tumbling off. An old woman at her doorstep sold me a couple of eggs, asking good-humouredly: "What! still here, you Germans? Don't you want to go back home, then? The war's lasted quite long enough … "

A staff-officer spoke to me more hopefully of the general situation. He said that it had come to the knowledge of the army commander that a rumour had gone round to the effect that we had been defeated and were in full retreat. That, he said, was entirely wrong: it was merely a question of the regrouping of units and reorganisation of the line for strategic reasons. He asked us officers to explain this to the men. Maubeuge, he added, had fallen, and we had taken twenty thousand French and English prisoners there and captured a mass of material.

In a village with the quaint name of Sacconin-et-Breuil there was a lengthy halt in a large farmyard; the towers, loopholes in the walls, and drawbridges and moat around, giving it the appearance of a fortress. We were informed that the regiment would be employed no longer as rear-guard to a strange division and was to rejoin its own. And then suddenly a car, covered in mud, drove in among us, and we recognised our corps commander, whom we had not seen since that evening at Hornu.

"Grenadiers!" he called out, standing up in his car, "I am glad to meet you again at last. I've not been able to get to you for a long time. When we were advancing you were always right in front: when we were retiring you were always right behind. But now all this miserable business of going backwards is over: we're going to turn round and show our teeth to the enemy." God! what a cheer greeted those words. "You have been badly knocked about and had heavy losses, but you've made history; and as I stand here in front of you I do not hesitate to say that the 12th Grenadier Regiment is the most efficient, reliable regiment in my corps. I will bring you to the notice of His Majesty. Good day to you, Grenadiers!" Tired arms lifted lines of dirty helmets into the air with shouting and cheering; and a fresh energy, a new spirit of defiance entered our failing hearts. Thank you, Papa Lochow.

The regiment then marched off again to join our own 5th Division: being "lent" to another was no fun at all. Below us, to our right front, lay the town of Soissons, with its old towers and gables. Suddenly a halt, a block in front. My company was still the last of the column, and a car drove up from behind with a general's flag on it; a white-moustached general got out and came up to me:

"What regiment is this?"

"12th Grenadiers, general."

"Where is your commander?"

"At the head of the regiment, sir."

"Well, I'm the commander of the Second Corps, and am responsible for the distribution of the troops assembling round Soissons. Will you ride on ahead to your commander and give him this order from me: "The 12th Grenadiers will move to Belleu and entrench there, facing south."

The ride was a difficult one, the road being filled with streams and cross-streams of men and guns and wagons. Finally I reached the colonel: he listened to the order unmoved, but for a brief moment a look of deep pity crossed his face: "My wretched men ... still no rest for them."

I returned to the company. On the outskirts of the town a long, strange procession was standing waiting. About a hundred Frenchmen in red képis in front, then as many English in their cloth caps and yellow-brown golfing-suits, and, at the tail, coloured men, all shades of colour from pale yellow to deepest black. The distinguished features of the Indians mixed with the gorilla faces of the negroes, a hotch-potch of nationalities, uniforms, and head-dresses which baffled my knowledge of ethnology. My company was astounded at the sight, greeting them with indignation and laughter.

"What's all that then, sir?" asked Sauermann. "Are they for Hagenbeck's Circus?"

"No, my lad, they're our enemies. Those are the people who have been brought together to save Europe and civilisation from the invasion of the Huns, the barbarians! And the Huns, the barbarians, are you and me, lad!"

"All the dirty lot ought to be killed, knocked over one after another!" growled my young man of Brandenburg.

I had a few words with a harmless, good-natured-looking French lieutenant, who complained of having no bread. "Bread!" I said. "Do you imagine we have any? We've hardly seen a crumb for two weeks." A young, handsome, and naïvely insolent English subaltern also asked for bread, and naturally got none. "Why didn't you stay at home on your island? What did you come here on the Continent for?"

"We were ordered to come, sir, and so we came. We are soldiers."

On, on! After climbing a steep hill we halted on the high ground among some woods. The major assembled the officers and said that owing to the heavy losses of the 1st and 2nd Battalions of the regiment they were to be formed into two companies each, instead of four, under Captain von Bülow and myself, the two companies taking the name of their leaders. The reorganisation was carried out, and I got my little crowd together: about 160 men out of the original 500!

It began to rain mercilessly, in sheets. My Grenadiers crept away under the trees, crouching there in groups, dejected and silent, others stood shivering under their overcoats, grumbling. "This is too bloody awful!" from one. "Can't go on any farther, it's more than a corpse could stand!" from another. I saw that something must be done to pull them together, to stop the rot of pessimism setting in. I made them all fall in under the dripping trees, and gave them a short sharp telling-off: "Look here, men, you've forgotten where you are! You seem to think you're on manoeuvres, that the 'cease fire' will sound at any moment, and all will be over. But this is war, lads. So far we've had amazing luck with the weather, and now when the first autumn storms arrive you whine like a lot of old women! Believe me, we've got much worse ahead of us. After the autumn comes winter, with snow and ice; have no doubt about that. This is only the beginning, so pull yourselves together!"

During the evening the regiment moved into the sheds and buildings of a brick factory nearby for the night. I was allotted a small cottage, which by the smell and the disorder of everything in it had obviously been used as a billet before: however, it had a roof and an oven. We had barely finished our meal when I was sent for by the major. I rode back behind the orderly for about a mile to battalion headquarters, which were in a very stately private house. Here I heard the latest news about our situation: the First Army was retiring across the Aisne, where it would take up a strong position on the northern bank and definitely hold up the enemy's advance from the south. The 5th Division, which had been covering the river crossings south of Soissons, was now to be withdrawn. Our 1st and 2nd Battalions were to cover the withdrawal during the night, Company Bloem to be responsible for the bridges near the sugar factory. "You will lead us there, Bloem."

Meanwhile the battalion had assembled, and was waiting in the road in utter darkness. I rode on ahead with my map and electric torch. After an hour and a half we reached the sugar factory. In front the Aisne flowed silently past, and on one of two wooden bridges, dimly lit by four lanterns, stood some engineer's. I sent patrols a short way upstream and downstream, leaving Lieutenant Chorus with his section in the sugar factory as the piquet, with a sentry-post under an NCO to guard the bridges themselves. The remainder of the company marched on across it to the north bank and halted near a small farm in St Paul, a suburb of Soissons, where they bivouacked.

It was about 3 am before I could get some sleep, lying booted and spurred on a very dirty bed in a miserable cottage: and here I dreamt for the first time a dream that was to disturb my sleep every night for weeks to come. I was lying in the middle of a big open field either wounded or exhausted, I never knew which, with my head lower than my feet: a battle was raging all around: shrapnel were screaming above me, machine-gun bullets were flicking into the earth at my side, shells were tearing enormous holes in the ground nearby, and then all of a sudden a noise of stamping, clattering, rattling approached me, and a battery of our heavy artillery drove heedlessly right over me – I lost consciousness and awoke with a hammering heart and panting for breath.

Daylight already. Good God! six o'clock. They must have all crossed the bridge by now. "Müssigbrodt, get my horse ready." I rode down to the bridge; the meadows on both banks of the Aisne were thick with dew, the river eddying under the bridge and flowing merrily along between them, a picture of perfect peace. Lieutenant Chorus reported that the night had passed uneventfully, nothing but an incessant stream of stragglers crossing the bridges: he had seen nothing of the 5th Division or the II Corps. I went back to the two sections in St Paul, the original D Company, under Lieutenants Löhmann and Wildegans: the men were cooking and foraging in the neighbouring orchards and kitchen-gardens, blissfully oblivious of the situation, which was getting more serious every minute. Looking across the valley one could see that the enemy's guns were already taking up a position on the wooded high ground by Belleu, where we had been the previous evening, and opening fire over the roofs of Soissons, evidently on to our new position along the northern side of the river. The II Corps must have crossed by the bridges at Soissons, and forgotten those at the sugar factory. The few engineers at the bridge had left, so I sent two cyclists to remind Engineer Headquarters at Soissons that the sugar-factory bridges were still intact, and then ordered Lieutenant Chorus to bring his men to the north side of the river. He waited till a cyclist returned from the engineer commandant with a message saying he was sending a party to blow up the bridge in ten minutes' time, and then I assembled the company and we marched off. Just after we started there was a tremendous explosion, evidently the bridges in the town being blown up, and shortly afterwards our wooden bridges at the sugar factory met the same fate.

I halted the company at Bucy-le-Long, in the park of a beautiful castle, and, going into it with the other officers, saw a sorry spectacle. Friend and foe had obviously used it as billets: the splendid furniture had been ruined or made into firewood for cooking, glasses and empty wine bottles all over the place, a valuable collection of historical costumes all torn to shreds, and an even more precious one of china broken to pieces; a revolting spectacle of wanton destruction.

We marched on again, turning north at Sainte Marguerite off the main road and up the valley of the Chivres brook. Here a cyclist from battalion headquarters met us with a message: "The 5th Division is assembling on the ridge south and south-west of Fort Condé." Following the winding road we passed through

Chivres village and on to the high ground above, joining up again there with the battalion.

In the course of the afternoon the whole regiment took up a position east of the winding road, and dug shelter-trenches. Though there was artillery-fire on all sides and in all directions, we ourselves were spared a shelling throughout the day. A violent storm with heavy rain came on at nightfall, and we put up our small bivouac tents close to the shelter-trenches, so as to be able to occupy them at once if necessary, Lieutenant Chorus and Sergeant Schüler sharing my tent. I got out my miniature hurricane-lamp, and by its candlelight our dog-kennel looked more comfortable. All at once the wet flap that formed the entrance was pulled aside, and there in the doorway crouched Ahlert: "I've found a bottle of wine for you, sir, and two cigars."

"You thrice-blessed angel! Where did you get them?"

"That's a secret, sir."

And so we all three lay together in our dripping-wet shelter, sipping the Burgundy as if each drop was of gold. Being the senior, the others insisted on my having a cigar to myself, while they smoked the other in turns. With light, wine, and cigars, our casino was so pleasant that we stayed awake till eleven. The wind and rain stormed incessantly outside, and the bombardment lasted all through the night, especially towards Soissons; and when I had a final walk along the row of bivouacs before turning in I saw the reflection in the sky above the town of a gigantic conflagration.

Chapter Eighteen

The Battle Of The Aisne And After

"Today's Sunday, sir: something's sure to happen!" my orderly remarked when he woke us the next morning. He was right. It was Sunday, September 13th. Tertre and Sancy were both on a Sunday.

During the morning, in anticipation of the coming artillery bombardment, the battalions were distributed on a wider front in better cover. Our own artillery was also taking up its positions, heavy and field batteries scattered about in every depression and behind every stretch of wood, their iron mouths raised high in the air and already spitting out their deadly poison across the valley. While looking for the new position, I happened to be passing near one of our heavy batteries when a gun suddenly fired. Not expecting it, I did not hold my ears soon enough, and the shock was like being hit with a big hammer on both sides of my head. I was practically deaf for the remainder of the day: my hearing, previously excellent, has never quite recovered from it.

At last a suitable position was found: a long strip of wood separated us from the Chivres valley and partly hid us from the enemy. We piled arms here and awaited the final order to entrench. Meanwhile the enemy's artillery had opened along the whole front, but uncertain of our actual positions he was firing at random over a wide area. Shortly after, the battalion adjutant came up and said the major wished to see me. We went through the strip of wood and found the major, Captain von Bülow, and the few remaining officers of the battalion standing in a clearing from which a grand view could be had across the valley. We could not see the Aisne itself, but a line of willows away on the far side marked its course, with here and there groups of houses and church towers along its green banks. Stretched out across the broad expanse of meadows between us and the river was a long line of dots wide apart, and looking through glasses one saw that these dots were infantry advancing, widely extended: English infantry, too, unmistakably.[1] A field battery on our left

---

1   This refers to the attack by the 12th Infantry Brigade (2nd Lancashire Fusiliers and the 2nd Essex Regiment); they had crossed the Aisne by the damaged bridge at Venizel, and thence attacked the Chivres spur and west of it. On their left the 1st Rifle Brigade (11th Brigade) had occupied the woods above St Marguerite, west of the Chivres valley, earlier in the day, having crossed the river during the night by the Venizel bridge, filing across the central girder which alone remained intact. The author of the *History of the Rifle Brigade*, 1914 – 1918, writes (p. 26): "Had the whole of the British advanced troops acted with the initiative and promptitude of the 11th Brigade, and established themselves swiftly on the high ground beyond the Aisne whilst the enemy was still fatigued and disheartened, the German line would probably have become untenable, and the Chemin des Dames would have fallen in the subsequent attack; there might have been a shattering German defeat. But the crossing was elsewhere postponed till daylight; and with daylight came artillery bombardment of the crossings, and a spirited attempt by the enemy to contest any further advance. The Battle of the Aisne, which began in earnest the following day, the 14th, was fought a day too late."

had spotted them, and we watched their shrapnel bursting over the advancing line. Soon a second line of dots emerged from the willows along the river bank, at least ten paces apart, and began to advance. More of our batteries came into action; but it was noticed that a shell, however well aimed, seldom killed more than one man, the lines being so well and widely extended. The front line had taken cover when the shelling began, running behind any hedges or buildings near by, but this second line kept steadily on, while a third and fourth line now appeared from the river bank, each keeping about two hundred yards distance from the line in front. Our guns now fired like mad, but it did not stop the movement: a fifth and a sixth line came on, all with the same wide intervals between men and the same distance apart. It was magnificently done.

The whole wide expanse of flat meadow-land beneath us was now dotted with tiny brown-grey men pushing on closer and closer, their attack obviously making for the position of the corps on our immediate right, from which rifle-fire was already hammering into the advancing lines. Nevertheless they still moved forwards, line after line of them, and gradually disappeared from our view behind the wooded slopes at the southern end of the Chivres valley.

We had watched the tactical excellence of this attack with such interest that we had forgotten we were standing in the open on the front edge of the very strip of wood that veiled our battalion's position from the enemy's view: a whole group of us in our light-grey, peace-time waterproofs with their red collars. The major suddenly realised it. "Gentlemen," he said, "we are damnably exposed here; a landmark for at least a couple of miles away! We'd better separate, and get more under cover." Scarcely had we moved away when four shrapnel burst and showered their contents all about the very place where all the officers of the battalion had been standing a minute before.

From now on the shelling of our position became constant, and on returning to my company I heard most sad news: that Lieutenant Wildegans, one of the very best, had been killed. I experienced once again that eternally incomprehensible sensation: the feeling of impossibility that a person with whom one has just been laughing and joking could suddenly lie there dumb and motionless for evermore. It appeared that he had been told of some bread in a bakery in Chivres village, and had gone there with Lieutenant Löhmann and a few men to claim it. He came out of the bakery door and had just shouted: "God, it's a wonderful find!" when a shrapnel burst above the group, smashing his helmet and his skull. So ended the life of this splendid fellow, always cheerful, and, in spite of his youth, loved and followed by his men as none other. Lieutenant Löhmann, too, and four men had been wounded by the same shell.

As the afternoon drew on the enemy's fire increased. The sun sent bright golden rays through the gaps in a heavy bank of black cloud, and to the east, high over the battle-field, lay a rainbow clear-cut against a slate-coloured sky.

A cyclist came up and handed me a large bag full of letters, letters from home! The first post we had had for fifteen days, since August 28th. Lying among my company, leaning on my elbows, I sorted out the letters, and they were passed round. For myself there was a whole packet, and among them seventeen letters from my wife. Seventeen letters! How many dark, wretched hours would they not help to brighten! Glancing at some of them, however, a sentence here and there an-

gered me: "The bells are ringing already, and flags are flying everywhere to celebrate another victory. How proud and happy you must be to be taking part in all
these wonderful successes … " But that was quite apart: it was my own home that I
wanted to hear about, after two weeks of horror, and now I was indeed blessed with
a regular flood of affection.

As I read a shell burst among the company: three men wounded, one with his
eye hanging down his cheek. Fortunately the battalion doctor was near at hand to
attend to them.

At last the order came to entrench; the position to be held "to the last man." By
nightfall we were well down into the stony ground, and were able also to bury the
dead, among them the well-beloved Wildegans. It was quite dark when all the officers of the battalion assembled round his grave. By the light of our electric torches
we had a last look at his rigid body, his forehead shattered, but still a smile on his
face, in spite of the deathly pallor. The major began to read a prayer, but his voice
faltered, and, too filled with emotion to continue, he stopped in the middle and
just murmured: "Amen." Amen! a bit of each of us lies buried there in that narrow,
stony grave.

I then returned to the trench and lay down in it with Sauermann, Niestrawski,
and Pohlenz. Ahlert came along with a blanket. I declined it, as the men had none.
"You must take it, sir. If any of us are ill, it will be useful. You must have it for our
sakes." So I gave in and kept the blanket.

Dawn came with a leaden sky heavy with rain. In the early hours a howitzer
battery took up a position close to our trenches, and we had to dig another line farther away. This new line was dug deep, and my "staff" made me my first dug-out;
that is to say, they laid cut saplings and thick branches across the top of the trench
and shovelled earth on them.

During the day the battle raged with renewed fury. The English attack we had
watched the previous afternoon had, we heard, penetrated deep into the position of
the neighbouring corps, as far as Vregny, though held up opposite Chivres village
by the 52nd Regiment. Nevertheless, the high ground on the far side of the Chivres
valley was in the enemy's possession, and English troops were in position within a
thousand yards of us, though hidden by the wood. So we sat in our dripping
trenches, the rain pouring down in torrents, hour after hour: crouching packed
close together, nibbling at the biscuits and chocolates and smoking the cigars received in our parcels from home the day before: and reading again and again those
letters; what bliss to have them to read! And all the time shells and bullets were
whistling, screaming above and about us, interspersed with the deafening discharges from our howitzer batteries close by.

It must have been about 11 am when I heard the major's voice in the trench
calling my name. I wriggled out of my "dug-out." "I've just got this order from the
colonel: 'The 1st Battalion of the 52nd Regiment,' he read, 'in position on the
southern slope and heavily engaged since yesterday, has successfully repulsed several strong English attacks, but with severe losses: our 1st Battalion will put a company at its disposal, which will move immediately and prolong the left of the line of
defence of the 52nd.' Your company is detailed for this," he added. "Is it quite
clear?"

"Yes, major."

I shouted as loud as I could along the trench, for the noise of the battle almost drowned one's voice: "Company Bloem in line, in front of the trench!"

Almost the first to clamber out was Grenadier Sukowski, close by me, and at that moment a shrapnel burst and emptied its load of bullets about us. Sukowski's face suddenly stiffened, and two small trickles of blood as thick as one's finger began to flow down his neck.

"Captain … ," he gurgled, "Capt … ," and I could see at once there was no hope for him.

"Sorry, lad, I can't help you," I said as he reached his hand out to me and I grasped it. He shivered convulsively and stared at me vacantly. Then the pressure of his hand weakened, his eyes became glassy, and he wavered. Niestrawski caught hold of him under his arms and let him collapse gently to the ground.

The company was now out of the trench. I glanced along the line: what a dirty lot of devils they looked, boots, coats, helmets, hands, beards, and rifles all smothered with a thick coating of mud and filth: but underneath their hearts were sound.

"Company – extend out – and advance on the wooden hut at edge of wood!" And forward we went across an open bit of hillside and then into the strip of wood that bordered the valley. In the middle of struggling through the dense undergrowth, Sauermann said: "The company isn't following us, sir!" and then a voice from behind called out: "Come back, sir!" I got back and saw the company moving away to the right along the wood-edge. A message was passed back that the company had to close in to the right, and that I was to go forward myself to the major commanding the battalion of the 52nd.

About ten minutes later I had found Major von Peschke, who was lying with his staff behind the somewhat doubtful protection of a stack of faggots. He told me my company was not required in the front line at the moment, but asked me to occupy a line of trench they had dug the previous day slightly in rear, in support.

When I returned to the company I noticed that Sergeant Schüler's section was missing. Evidently they had gone into the thick undergrowth of the wood and the order had not reached them. A pity, but they would find their way back to us all right.

We followed a broad, grassy ride through the wood, along which a blood-spattered, staggering procession of wounded men were coming from the front. On reaching the further side was a line of trench, and the whole place here lay under heavy artillery- and rifle-fire, shells and bullets whistling through the leaves and cracking branches like an autumn wind. In front of one part of the trench was a big pile of logs, hollowed out underneath to form a kind of dug-out. Three orderlies sat inside chatting, but the master of the house stood behind, out in the open, his hands sunk deep in his coat-pockets, calmly smoking a cigarette. It was Captain von Alvensleben, commanding A Company of the 52nd.

"Hullo, Alvensleben."

"Morning, Bloem. What are you doing here?"

I explained to him. "And you?"

"Battalion reserve. Have a cigarette?"

"Gladly. A thousand thanks."

We talked, and I kept wondering why he didn't go into the dug-out. As he remained outside I naturally did too, and we watched the continuous stream of wounded coming back and passing on along the ride. Now a man alone, his eyes terribly swollen and his right arm smashed and held between the buttons of his blood-stained overcoat. Now two together supporting each other, followed by another using his rifle as a crutch. Then another wretched fellow with his arm completely shattered below the shoulder, a round bleeding hole with a bit of flesh and cloth hanging from it: he was holding the useless lower part of the arm, still in its sleeve, pressed to his side with his left hand. He passed by, stunned, stupefied, staring with bent head at the round bleeding hole that had once been the upper part of his arm.

This ghastly procession appalled me; and yet as the callous Alvensleben stood there chatting away and smoking completely unmoved, I made no comment and changed the subject. "A few days ago at Sancy," I said, "I was lying alongside a company of your regiment under artillery-fire. Its commander must be a pretty tough nut." And I related how he had thrown things at my messenger's head when I'd passed on the order to retire.

"That was me," said Alvensleben. "Have another cigarette?"

The shrapnel were bursting right and left of us, all round us. Why on earth didn't he go into the dug-out? Suddenly he shouted out: "Damn it! Look at that fool Kramer, again with more than he can carry: he makes me tired: go and help him, you fellows!" Out of the wood came an NCO with a badly wounded man on his back, stumbling and tumbling over with the weight of him. We all went and helped to bring the wounded man and his rescuer into the dug-out. I assisted in bandaging him, but Alvensleben was already outside again. We finished, and I was about to join him when a shell burst just above the pile of logs, some of the bullets ricocheting through, one grazing my shoulder. I cursed, but its force was already spent and my arm was unhurt, though numbed for a moment.

"You see!" said Alvensleben. "Come outside again; it's much pleasanter out here."

A messenger came up. "Major von Peschke wishes to see you, sir." I went back with him.

"They've had such losses in the front line, Bloem, that I want you to go up closer. So take your company on until you are in touch with Detering's company. Find some cover there and wait until he asks you to support him. I want Detering to feel he has support close at hand."

I thought for a moment. "Have I time, major, to go forward myself first to see the position and find a suitable place? Then the company could follow on."

"Certainly, there's no hurry."

Picking up Sauermann and Niestrawski on the way I followed the path into the wood beyond. As we went on through it towards the front line the fury of the battle increased. To right and left, in front and behind, were little puffs of white smoke above and among the trees as the shrapnel burst and sent their load of shot rattling down on to the path and against the tree-trunks: the noise was as a strong wind howling among the tree-tops, and yet the day was calm and still. Bullets buzzed and hummed through the branches as if a swarm of thousands of locusts had invaded the wood, and a continual rain of twigs and leaves floated to earth. The high explosive shells hurtled through, burrowing deep into the sodden ground like blows from a colossal steam-hammer: the earth itself seemed to crack, and masses of smoke, bits of rock, clods of mud, and large chips of shell shot up into the air: now and again these monsters would undermine a tree, the explosion uprooting it and sending it twirling like a corkscrew through the air till it fell in a million splinters. A monotonous and incessant rumbling like the beating of a monster kettledrum in the distance formed the bass of the battle symphony. This and the screaming in the wood about me were constant, never-ceasing, but between the high notes and the low notes was a mad confusion of deafening uproar: like the yelpings of a giant dog gone mad and the rocks of the hills being burst asunder.

In the oncoming darkness the whole wood appeared utterly bewitched as I passed on through it with my two followers close behind. And as I went, with death as it were at my side about to strike at any moment, I again felt that amazing thrill of indescribable bliss born of the courage that conquers bodily fear, an ecstasy such as I had never experienced nor even suspected within my reach before the war. All my ambitions, my hopes, my work became trivial, were as nought: and in renouncing them a great sense of release, of salvation came over me. I felt that my failings were pardoned, and that all those I had harmed in any way had forgiven me. So, too, had one whose hand I now felt on my shoulder. I spoke to him: "Take me, I am ready."

And he answered me in a voice I did not recognise but in words that were familiar to me since childhood: "A thousand shall fall at thy left hand, and ten thousand at thy right, but it shall not come nigh thee." And these words became a song which gradually grew and swelled into a mighty anthem, a pæan of triumph by a many thousand-throated choir of sweetest angelic voices, at times fading away, so soft as to be scarcely audible, then rising grandly and strongly again to a full massed chorus of rejoicing. And the rumbling ebb and flow of the monstrous orchestra in wood and valley was the accompaniment to this psalm of thanksgiving.

Never before nor since have I experienced so intensely the joy of sacrifice, of surrendering things temporal for things eternal, but I now know how sweet and glorious it is. And I know, too, that if this is its prelude, then death must be merely as a joyous home-coming after an aimless journey.

The wood now began to slope more steeply down to the valley. Across the path and in the undergrowth alongside lay more and more dead bodies, men who had taken their last step in this terrible march, so many that in the failing light one had to be careful to avoid stumbling on them. Surely the position of the 52nd could not be much farther. I shouted at the top of my voice: "Captain Detering! Captain Detering!"

"Here!" came an answering call from the right, and we groped our way through the wood towards each other. I told him my orders.

"Splendid! Come along and see where we are. Two of my sections, or rather all that's left of them, are entrenched just ahead along the low side of the wood: I've only this moment come back from them, and was going to settle down with my reserve section for the night. It's not particularly comfortable, but there's probably room for you all."

We came to a quarry cut into the wooded hillside, cliff-like rocks jutting out on both sides of it. In the front part of it lay ten dead, and farther in was the section, much depleted, with its commander, Lieutenant Zeidler, with a bandaged hand. There seemed just room for my men, so I sent Sauermann back for them.

The ravine gave a very passable protection, but with the oncoming night the shelling and firing had slackened. We smoked and I listened to the account of the desperate English attacks that had taken place and of the heavy losses on both sides. Our own brigade – General Sontag's – appeared to have suffered terribly. Eventually my lads arrived, all unhurt, though Schüler's section was still absent, and they settled down as best they could with the others.

Our conversation was suddenly interrupted by a confused uproar on the high ground behind us. A few shots followed by rousing cries and shouting, and then wild cheers and hurrahs. What on earth could it be? Had they broken through and were now fighting behind us? Impossible. After a few moments the strange tumult stopped, and the night was at peace again. Not quite! for we had a final good-night from the enemy: a rafale from all his guns simultaneously.

"The English aren't going to work overtime to-night, then!" said Niestrawski; but the words were hardly out of his mouth when, damn it! a flash just above our heads, a crash, a cry, and a groan ... A shrapnel, sent with the enemy's blessing, had hit a tree above us, burst, and shed its contents over us. Only two wounded, which was lucky in the circumstances: but they were severe cases, one hit through the lung, and when I flashed my electric torch into his chalk-white face, blood was already pouring from his mouth. I bound up the wound as well as I could: he was moaning pitifully.

"Captain ... captain ... I'm dying – I shall die."

"Nonsense, lad. Lung wounds heal up in no time. If you were going to die, you'd be dead by now." He would have to stay where he was for the night, but rest was what he most needed.

The other had the whole of the calf of his left leg torn away by a piece of shell-casing. It was difficult to dress, and took at least ten bandages.

There were two hundred live men sharing the quarry with ten dead, and we lay on the damp, rocky ground packed like sardines in a tin. My head was between two dirty hob-nailed boots, and between my knees was a helmeted head, a pack, and the upper part of a heavily breathing body. I was trying hard to sleep when my name was called. I answered, and there, close by, among the confusion of legs and bodies, stood three or four men of the missing section of Sergeant Schüler, all trying to speak to me at once, and gesticulating wildly.

"We've got them, sir! we gave them something to think about!"

"We took four prisoners and the others put up a fight, but we killed them."

"Not one of them got away, sir, not a single one." And so they jabbered on, a babble of chatter as if they'd gone crazy or were drunk.

"Children, I don't understand a word you're saying. Grandert, just pull yourself together and tell me quietly what has happened." Even then it was difficult to get a clear picture, but I gathered that as soon as Schüler found he had lost touch with the company, he had got his section together and wandered all over the place looking for us. All of a sudden in the middle of a wood they came across a number of English soldiers, and Schüler, without a moment's hesitation, ordered his men to fix bayonets and charge. This they did, shouting and cheering as they ran forward. A desperate hand-to-hand fight took place for a couple of minutes, during which four Englishmen were taken prisoners and the rest, about thirty all told, killed.[2]

"And where's Sergeant Schüler?" I asked.

"He's badly wounded, and Sergeant Döring, too. We carried them back, sir."

Good God! two more of my best NCO's gone. Chorus was now the only section commander I had left of the two combined companies. It was past midnight before the rest of Schüler's section were got together and lay down where they could, but they talked on incessantly, describing to the others what they'd missed. "Be quiet, children, and go to sleep. It's after midnight, and you'll want all your strength for tomorrow."

I had almost dozed off when I was wakened again. In the midst of the pile of bodies, of which mine was one, stood Ahlert.

"Good Heavens! What in the name of all the devils are you doing here?"

"The cooker is here, sir."

"Are you mad? Where?"

"On the path, about ten minutes back. And here's a little extra for you, sir, a bit of fresh sausage Elberling has made specially."

"But it's madness, Ahlert, to bring the cooker right up to the front line like this. One shot into the container, and good-bye dinners."

"All the same, the company must have something to eat, sir. Who knows when they'll be able to get another meal?"

"You're right. Well, we must get them up somehow and take them along to fill up." Waking the men and getting them along in the pitch-dark back to the cooker was no easy matter. But God! how they tucked in once they were there. How excellent the hot soup tasted, and the boiling coffee, and that bit of sausage! My good Elberling, your sausages are worthy of a poem to themselves.

At last we were back in the quarry again with warm, contented stomachs, and before long a hundred and sixty men were peacefully snoring all around me. At last, too, sleep came to me. Good night, my loved ones, far away over there. I'm still alive, still living for you. "A thousand shall fall at thy left hand, and ten thousand at thy right, but it shall not come nigh thee."

Zola, describing the awakening of the French soldiers on the morning of Sedan, says they were "terror-stricken at the thought of being still alive." And yet a battle in those days only lasted eight hours, while here were we by no means terror-stricken and still ready for anything, a band of hardened old veterans.

At dawn, before the battle had opened again, I reorganised the sections: Lieutenant Chorus kept to his, Döring's men I gave to Corporal Boettcher, and Schüler's to young Corporal Esche. I had no senior NCO's left. Schüler, I heard, had died during the night in the dressing-station at Fort Condé. How difficult to

2   These were almost certainly a party of the 1st Norfolk Regiment. The History of this Regiment states: "On September 14th the brigade (15th) had orders to clear the spur leading down from the north and having on it the Condé fort ... After 4.30 pm a mixed force of twelve companies went forward to attack the spur ... Twenty-five men and two officers of the 1st Norfolk appear to have got far forward into the wood, where both the officers were killed, and the rest either taken prisoner or killed. These were of 'C' Company."

believe that I should never see his honest face again. One after the other they were leaving; and they were the best I had.

Shortly afterwards a message came from Major von Peschke. Firstly: "Send back an orderly to take messages when required." I sent Sauermann. Secondly: "There is a gap between the 1st and 2nd Battalions of the 52nd Regiment through which the English came yesterday evening, but fortunately they were all killed or taken prisoners. It is at the point of the wood opposite Missy village, and Company Bloem will advance into the front line to make good this gap."

"Lieutenant Chorus, do you understand that? Then will you take your section there?"

"Yes, sir." And as he put his hand to his helmet to salute, I noticed behind the large spectacles he wore a strangely solemn look in his eyes. It was as if they were saying: "Some disaster will happen to me today"; but before I could realise it he had turned, extended his section, and was disappearing into the dense undergrowth of the wood.

It was not long before a man came back and handed me a cartridge-case, inside which was a rolled-up note: "I'm being enfiladed by a heavy fire from Missy village. Please send reinforcements to prolong my right. Chorus."

Right. "Boettcher, fall in your section, and I will go with you. Esche, you stay here with yours in reserve." Our way led us along past the front line of the 52nd. There they were kneeling or standing in a line of deep holes they'd dug, one, two, or even three in a hole. They had been there now for three days with scarcely anything to eat or drink, and engaged continuously. The dead had been lifted out of the holes and were lying alongside – stiff and dumb companions for those still living. I passed two company commanders, Rehm and Leonhard, sitting smoking in holes behind the centre of their companies, and occasionally looking towards a village that stood up like a miniature fortress in the Aisne valley in front. It was Missy, from where the whole line was being enfiladed.

I found Chorus already laid out on the ground, his coat covered with blood from a shot through the shoulder. "Bear up! As soon as we can stop this fire you'll be taken back." Above, to the right, a great mass of rock projected out from the wood, from which it seemed that one could fire right into the position of these damned Englishmen: that would stop them enfilading our line for a bit anyhow.

We moved off at once back into the wood, and climbing up my one prayer was for a good position. On the way we stumbled on a dead English soldier in the undergrowth, his skull split open: then another, a bent bayonet deep into his breast: then a whole heap – of them together, evidently the over-bold invaders of our position the previous evening, and the victims of my much-lamented Schüler and his section. It gave us fresh confidence to see some dead enemy again. The ascent was steep and the undergrowth so dense that each had to work and wriggle his own way through, but at last we came into the open again: had we found the position?

We stood on a terrace of rock jutting out like a bastion from the hillside, high above the Aisne valley that lay at our feet bathed in sunshine, and there, straight in front, scarcely six hundred yards away, was a flat-topped ridge rising up from the meadows of the valley, and crowning it was, the village of Missy. The houses were built in the French manner, side by side in one long street, and we overlooked the backs of those on the northern side, with their gardens, sheds, and outhouses facing us. In the centre an ancient church-tower bid us defiance, while on the left was a small citadel, and by it the cemetery surrounded by a stone wall, overshadowed by a row of oak trees. From there and from the length of the village came a hammering of machine guns and an incessant rifle-fire. They were in the village right enough somewhere, but that was all one could say.[3] I told the men to creep forward to the edge of the terrace of rock, finding a good rest for their rifles, and then we'd show them what we could do.

On either side of me lay Corporal Scheumann, a dentist by profession, and Grandert: while beyond them was Niestrawski and Pohlenz. The English had not yet seen us, and, as we could hear, were still enfilading the line of trenches below to our left. Just wait, you devils, first of all we'll stop that nasty little trick of yours. Now, lads, a few volleys to start with, at random into the village, just to show the blackguards they've got another enemy in front of them and give our friends below a rest. Take your time from me.

"At the houses in the village, sights 600 yards – Aim! Fire!! – Load! Aim! Fire!! – Load! Aim! Fire!! – Load! Now fire in your own time."

We had no sooner fired the three volleys than our skilled opponents had spotted our exact position and were answering us, the bullets whistling about our ears, striking the rock beneath with a sharp crack, and hitting the trees above, breaking off twigs and leaves that showered down on us. "Cease fire!" and by drawing slightly back we were covered by the ledge of rock. We had drawn their attention, and the next thing was to find just where the scoundrels were lying. My neighbours and I pushed ourselves forward so as to be able to see the village, and in a few moments suggestions were coming from right and left.

"Look, sir, in that garden by the red house to the right of the church! I can see two brown hats quite clearly."

"Have a shot then, Grandert – I'll watch through my glasses." No result. Naturally, I couldn't see the strike of the bullet, but neither could I see any brown hat.

"There, sir!" Niestrawski called out excitedly. "In the church tower: someone just moved in that window."

"Quite possible! All four of you then, have one round at the church-tower window." And through my glasses I saw the window panes smash.

Another said he'd seen a head peering out of the skylight in the roof of the second red house to the left of a large prominent tree. It too was fired at, and a number of slates rattled down from the roof.

---

3   To quote from the *British Official History*, p. 369: "The Germans at the end of the Chivres spur offered a stout resistance ... The 13th Infantry Brigade found it impossible to move along the road towards Condé, which was swept by the German artillery and could not therefore reach its assigned position to assail the Chivres spur from the southeast. Thus the whole movement was checked. The rear battalions of the 15th Infantry Brigade and the Cornwall LI of the 14th became crowded together in Missy village, and a German aeroplane passing over the village took note of this congestion. At 10 am the German artillery poured such a storm of shells upon the houses that the battalions were compelled for a time to evacuate the village. Gradually they returned to their original places in it, always under harassing fire from German snipers at the edge of the wood, and there they remained till dark."

Damn it! I could see something myself. "Look, lads! behind that pile of wood by a small shed at the right end of the village – close to the road. Two Englishmen! Do you see them? I can see them now with my naked eye."

"Which shed do you mean, sir?" There were indeed dozens of sheds near the road, and most of them had piles of logs by them, but I couldn't describe it any clearer.

"Lend me your rifle a minute, Scheumann." Taking careful aim I fired.

"Now you see which shed I mean." An Englishman jumped up from behind the pile of logs and ran with long strides towards the village street. They all fired at him, but he was soon behind the houses. By the log-heap, however, lay another, stiff and motionless. My aim had been true – the hunter's greeting!

But this was a waste of time. We had drawn the enemy's fire and stopped, temporarily at any rate, the enfilading of the trenches below us; but we could do little with our rifles against such a well-concealed enemy. If only one could get into communication with our artillery; a few heavy shells into the village, and that would settle the matter.

Corporal Boettcher, the section leader, proposed firing at the wall of the cemetery: he had seen some heads behind it. "All right! Two rounds everyone at the top of the cemetery wall. Take careful aim." The effect was amazing. For a moment after the shots the enemy's fire weakened considerably; but after a pause it began again, and we drew back under cover of the rock. Then forward again, a round or two at the cemetery wall and back again. So it went on, like a game of hide-and-seek for about half an hour, but nothing much could be expected of it. If only the guns knew – !

And then suddenly something tremendous, invisible and uncanny, hurtled screaming above our heads – thank the Lord, our heavies at last! A second later a gigantic column of black smoke rose in the air to the right of the village, by the end house, and immediately afterwards the roar of the explosion reached our ears. Hurrah! If only one could tell them to range more to the left … Wschlwschlwschlwschlwschl – another rent the air above us and rrms! – fifty yards further to the left, but short this time – in a field and thirty yards this side of the houses. Rrms! – crash! A third, right into the middle of the village – an entire house, a mass of splinters and debris, was lifted into the air. "They can see all right, those gunners! and they'll make things hum in that village quicker than we can."

Shell after shell followed in quick succession. Systematically from right to left they combed the village, the fate of a house being sealed by almost every shell. If only they'd try a little more to the left – on that cemetery wall at the extreme end of the place. Wschlwschlwschlwschlwschl – rrms! rrms! God! they've got it – two right into the cemetery, the coal-black fumes spurting up above the tops of the oak-trees.

"Look, sir, look! There they are, they're running!" shouted six, ten voices simultaneously. True enough they were streaming away, whole groups of them out of the cemetery and into the village. I jumped to my feet, we all jumped up to see better and to fire standing from our rocky bastion into the horde of running Britons.

Damn! a crash right among us, stinking fumes, a blow from behind against the back of my left knee as if the whole of the lower part of my thigh had been torn clean away from my leg. I staggered two or three steps to one side: "Down, lads! For God's sake, lie down!" – a round lump of lead, probably a shot from the shrapnel that had hit my knee, rolled over the rock-edge into the valley below. I got down and felt my leg. A circular hole through the stout leather-covering between the knees of my riding-breeches showed the track of the shot, but the leg itself was all right, stiff and hurting like blazes, but the bones were sound. I cursed loudly and well, though it might have been much worse; our own damned silly fault after all, for jumping up and standing firing in the open like that.

"Is it all right, sir?" Some of the men had seen and crawled towards me, looking anxiously at me.

"It's nothing, children! All's well! A bit of shrapnel in the back of the knee, that's all. Now, we'll get forward again to the edge and go on firing." I got forward and had the butt of my rifle against my cheek ready to aim when a sudden faintness overcame me. The village and landscape seemed to move away into the far, far distance, a glassy film dimmed my eyesight, blurring everything about me, and then, in spite of myself, I rolled on my back: "Hold me, children – "

Five or six rushed to me: "You're quite pale, sir – you've been hit ... " and I began to sink quite peacefully, contentedly, comfortably into the soft, vast depths of unconsciousness. And I dreamt a dream, indescribably vivid and yet so confused and disordered that I do not remember it. I only know I had it, and into it came the words, very faintly at first then more and more perceptible: "Sir! Sir! Captain Bloem! Yes, he's coming round! He's waking!" – and then I awoke. A dozen and more wildly unkempt, familiar, and much-loved faces were bending over me, full of anxiety. They had taken off my coat and shirt, and Scheumann, the dentist, was rubbing my chest. I felt a hot, clammy dampness round my left thigh, and my right arm was throbbing above the elbow. I unbraced my riding-breeches, and found the shirt and drawers simply soaked with blood. In a moment Scheumann found the wound: "You've been hit in the thigh by a rifle-bullet as well!" True: it had gone in in front and made a bigger wound at the back, and a similar trace of it was seen through the breeches. Scheumann bandaged it up. "Might have been much worse," he added. "Only just missed the bone and the main artery – "But it was all one to me. I was too dizzy, faint beyond caring.

"Right, that's done. Now, let's have a look at the arm." Here, too, a bullet had passed clean through, but nothing serious: it was painful to bend, one of the extension muscles must have been cut and that's all. Evidently I had been hit by two rifle-bullets simultaneously with the strike of the shrapnel at the back of my knee and with the greater shock of the latter had not felt the other two wounds.

I knew I could go on with the fight no longer. Eight strong hands lifted me up. "Corporal Boettcher – I hand over command of the company to you."

"Yes, sir," and a look of deep pride crossed his face. I never saw him again; he was severely wounded in the autumn fighting in the Champagne and died in a hospital in Germany after much suffering.

As they carried me away I looked back at the line of figures lying along the edge of the rocky bastion about to open fire again. They waved at me and waved – and I felt a stifling, incomprehensible pain within me, tearing at me – many of my heart-strings snapped at that moment.

"Just hold me under the arms, lads, and I'll try and hobble along. That's better." Niestrawski, Pohlenz, Grandert, and Scheumann stayed with me, helping me through the wooded undergrowth, over rocks and masses of boulders. The English sent their farewell greetings bursting all about us as we passed the rigid, contorted corpses of their friends, Schüler's victims, again. Then on past the trenches of the 52nd, where Captain Rehm gave me a drink of brandy from his flask to help me on: and Schmidthuis, now commanding Chorus's section, came up and said they had been all right as soon as we stopped the enfilade fire from Missy. But I saw and heard all this as through a mist. Now we were by the quarry, and there was Detering and his subaltern, Zeidler, and Corporal Esche with my reserve section. No sooner had we stopped here for a moment's rest than I was away once more, deep, deep into the vast spaces of oblivion.

When I came to again, I told Grandert and Scheumann to go back to their section, where they would be badly missed, and thanked them with all my heart for their kindness and care. I never saw them again. Both lie buried near Arras.

Niestrawski and Pohlenz now held me, one under each arm, and we continued our weary march. I could almost walk alone now, and without pain, but I was unsteady and all my strength had left me. Limping along the wooded path up the hillside we came to the place from where I had watched the procession of wounded, and then through the wood in which the angelic choir had sung their heavenly anthem. No shells were bursting in it, no shrapnel, only an occasional rifle-bullet humming through the tree-tops. But the many silent bodies, their faces now violet-tinted, and the countless trees, smashed, uprooted, lying at all angles about the wood, still remained as a reminder of the horrors of the previous evening.

Good! now we were on the top, on the flat, we could get along better. There, in front of us through the trees, we could see Fort Condé: and above it, fluttering in the sunshine, a large, white flag with a red cross. The enemy's range-finders must have been able to spot this flag at least three miles off, but that made no difference to the English: they kept the fort and the ground around it under constant artillery-fire. Possibly they thought we were using it as a headquarters and that the flag was just a fraud, but they were wrong: it was a dressing-station and field-hospital, nothing more nor less.

Before running the gauntlet through this belt of fire we stopped for a rest in an empty shelter-trench, and it was here that Colonel von Lotterer, the brilliant commander of our artillery brigade, came and spoke to me. He most kindly took a sympathetic interest in a humble captain of infantry; but I hardly saw his face, for my eyes were riveted on his breast, where he was wearing what I now looked upon for the first time – the Iron Cross of 1914.

I knew that I had been twice recommended for it, after the Battle of Mons and after Sancy, but I had not yet seen it; and now of a sudden there it was, and the sight of the black-and-white ribbon stirred me beyond words.

Two stretcher-bearers passed, and feeling exhausted I accepted their offer to carry me the rest of the way on the stretcher. But it was far from comfortable, at times it was even excruciatingly painful, and as we approached the fort and into the shell-zone I told them to stop. There were now four men with me, and a direct hit would kill all four for my sake. I declined the responsibility, had myself taken off the stretcher, sent the bearers on ahead, and then followed, supported as before by my two faithful "staff." They made most horrible jests about the shells, but I was not in a mood for them. Moreover, I noticed an amazing change in my outlook now that I was wounded: All my former worldly desires and ambitions, my buried selfishness, had come to life again. Not only was I no longer a piece of a living, struggling, wounded Germany, but I even ceased to be interested in anything unless it concerned my own miserable little scrap of life. I'd got my two wounds, enough and to spare, and all I thought of now was to avoid being shot dead as well. Rrms! another high-explosive, twenty yards ahead: uprooting a tree and sending it splintering into matchwood, sky-high. Damn you, you swine! Stop your infernal, everlasting din! I simply couldn't stand it any more. I – simply – couldn't – go – on. Somehow, my two faithful supporters pulled me on, over shell-holes, and through a wood of shattered tree-trunks, no leaves, no branches, like rows of tree-corpses, still standing but lifeless.

At last we reached the fort and entered by a high-arched passage that led down under twenty feet of earth. Thank heaven for that, we were safe! I now had to part with Niestrawski and Pohlenz. I shook their hands, I thanked them more than words could say for their unbounded goodness to me on that day and on all the other days we had spent together. Their loyalty was one of the most treasured memories I had of those turbulent, terrible, yet glorious weeks. Tears welled up into their eyes. "In six weeks at the most, lads, I'll be with you again."

But I have not seen them again, those truest of the true: and I shall never, never see them again. We shall never meet in after years and talk, over our cups, of our triumphal march together through Belgium and France, of that sudden change in the fortunes of war and our sulky and defiant retreat, and of our even more defiant stand on the rocky bastion near Fort Condé. Niestrawski lies buried in the valley of the Aisne not far from Missy, and Pohlenz away somewhere in Russia. Never, never shall I see them again.

Strange how still it was now all round me: after many days the noise and traffic of battle had suddenly ceased. A friendly assistant-doctor relieved me of my blood-soaked underclothing, and dressed my wounds, and on hearing my name brought one of the head doctors, Krüger-Franke, to see me. We had been at the same university, and from then on I was treated like a prince. Instead of a bed in the casemates of the fort I was bedded down in the doctor's own sitting-room, a very dirty one, but very peaceful: all I could possibly want in the way of refreshment was brought to me and washed down with a bottle of claret, followed by a cigar beyond price, a gift in memory of our university.

Later I was visited by a friend in the 18th Field Artillery Regiment, Captain Nitschmann, who had also been wounded in the leg, and limped in on a stick. "I wanted to tell you I have a small farm-cart coming along from my battery this evening, if the English leave us alone, to take me back to rail-head. I'm sick of this fort; there's no room left, and it's time we cleared out. Besides, the English may break through; they're at Vregny already – and to be taken by them, wounded – no thanks. Will you come with me?"

"Certainly I will. You needn't fear a breakthrough. I've just come from the front line, and they'll hold all right. But every step back will take me nearer home, and that's my next objective!"

At nightfall the shelling ceased, and in pouring rain the doctors helped us both into the rickety little cart. Behind us walked a procession of three hundred lightly wounded, and a mounted sergeant of Nitschmann's battery who knew the road led the way. Two hours through sheets of rain, black night, and shell-holes, every jolt giving an electric shock through my wounded limbs, brought us to Nanteuil. And there Ahlert met me, with Willy Weise and Müssigbrodt, all of them back looking after the company wagons and transport, also Elberling and Liebsch, the company butchers. We had quarters in a comfortable house, were fed and cared for like sick children, and slept like gods.

The next morning, with the help of a strong stick Müssigbrodt had found for me, I hobbled across to a house nearby, where I heard Chorus was lying. He was very feeble and in great pain; his arm could never be used again, but I gathered he would recover. After that we got up into our rickety cart, and I watched through a mist of tears the last of my grey company waving and cheering me as we moved off. "Good luck, I'll be with you again in six weeks!"

Our farm-cart rolled merrily on, but at a walking pace, for behind us still limped the procession of the three hundred with bandaged heads and arms. By my side in the cart was a large, black wicker-basket containing the final proof of Ahlert's care, a last gift of B Company to its captain: a loaf of bread, a bottle of red wine, and an enormous fresh sausage, one of Elberling's masterpieces. Nitschmann, too, had collected enough captured tins of English bully-beef to last us both home.

We were now out of range of the enemy's guns; and looking back, not without difficulty and pain, we could see the long lines of the little, white puffs of cloud, the shrapnel-bursts, hanging over the Aisne valley. But the peculiar thing was that the further we went along our road, north-westwards, the clearer could we hear the roar of another battle in front. A battle behind us and a battle in front of us! Only one explanation was possible, that the enemy was trying to envelop our right wing; and supposing he had? The whole district we were passing through was completely empty. Only eight miles behind the Aisne battlefront, and yet not a sign of a soldier, a wagon, a car – nothing. It seemed, indeed, as if the thin line now resisting the enemy's counter-offensive had not the slightest support, no reserves anywhere.

Our progress was exceedingly slow. About midday we met a transport column, and its commander handed us over one hundred and fifty loaves of bread for the procession of the three hundred. We halted by the side of a wood and had the meal of a king. Bless you, Elberling!

On, on again, past Coucy-le-Chateau, a gigantic ruin standing proudly on a high ridge to our right. With every mile the battle noise behind us got less and less, while that in front, somewhere about Noyon we thought, became louder and louder. It was dusk by the time our cart finally jolted through the cobbled streets of Chauny, and it was an eye-opener for us front-line soldiers to see the comfortable, easy life of the troops on the lines of communication: the supply depots, engineer and bridge-train parks, medical service companies, all looking well washed, happy, and well fed. This, too, was rail-head, with a real railway in operation under German administration.

At the railway-station we heard further news of the situation. It was a fact that the enemy had tried to get round our right wing, but he was being held, and the XV

Corps was now hurrying with all speed by rail from Lorraine to meet the danger. Every available reserve had been gathered together and sent out to guard the threatened flank, and the battle had been raging about Noyon since early morning.

We hobbled on to the platform where a long train was waiting for the transport of wounded: no comfortable hospital train in those days, but mainly cattle-trucks with straw to lie on, and into these the three hundred were packed in addition to a number of prisoners. We officers were more fortunate, being lifted into a first-class compartment of a proper carriage, and there we heard the incredible: bright, cheery women's voices speaking German, and at our door appeared three German nurses.

"Why are you so far back? Away in front, that's where we wanted you … "

"But we aren't allowed – we would go so gladly if we could … "

The train was due to start at 6 pm, but at 7 pm it was still standing at the platform. More wounded kept streaming in from the Noyon front, and the cattle-trucks were already filled to overflowing. A Hussar lieutenant joined us in our compartment: he'd had a shrapnel-shot in his neck, still there, and his grey cavalry-coat was literally smothered in blood. In a hoarse voice, scarcely comprehensible, he told us he could neither eat, drink, nor even swallow, and yet within five minutes he was sharing our red wine, sausage, and bully-beef with an almost alarming appetite and thirst.

Eight pm, and the train still waiting by the platform. The station-master came along and told us we could settle down for the night, as the enemy's cavalry had got through and blown up the railway bridges over the Crozat Canal beyond Tergnier. An armoured train with railway engineers was already on its way there to make a temporary bridge in their place.

A jolly thought to go to sleep with: surrounded by the enemy, cut off from home, wounded, defenceless, and crammed in a train with about a thousand wounded and three hundred prisoners. However, we settled down for the night and slept, and my slumber was again disturbed by that same nightmare I had dreamt so constantly at the front.

The bustle on the platform woke us early. Doctors came and dressed our wounds again. Orderlies brought along baskets of bread; and nurses, laughing and joking, handed round coffee, cigarettes, and chocolates. Suddenly there was a commotion, people rushing hither and thither, and shouting: in a couple of minutes the whole station was empty: a nurse running past called to us that there was an alarm; that Chauny was being attacked from the north.[4]

The prisoners were ordered out of the trucks and marched away into the town between rows of men with fixed bayonets: no one seemed to worry about the wounded, we were left to look after ourselves.

Yes, there it was! the booming of guns to north of us, and distant rifle-firing. "Well, Bloem, you know what's going to happen next," said Nitschmann. "Very soon some French cavalry gentlemen will come along, and say: 'Descendez, messieurs, et suivez-nous!' And no matter whether we are halt, lame, or blind, they will neither ask nor care."

---

4   This refers to French cavalry raids. It was the preliminary to that operation known as the "Race to the Sea," that culminated in the First Battle of Ypres.

Three hours went by, three hours almost more nerve-racking than being under shell-fire, when of a sudden, with a jerk and without the slightest warning, the train moved. It went out of the station, past the houses of the town into the open country, and then as suddenly stopped again. Ten minutes passed, it moved on, stopped, and then on again, this time really on as if it meant it.

Gradually we left the noise of battle behind, and passing through Tergnier Station very slowly came to the canal. The armoured train was in a siding, and the railway engineers had excelled themselves. They had made a bridge of pontoons above the blown-up bridge, floated it down and anchored it to the wreckage, then piled masses of logs and sleepers on the pontoons up to the level of the embankment on either side, placed a couple of rails along the top, and there was the bridge ready. In peace-time no one in his senses would have sent an engine across it with even a dead dog on board, but now in war-time a thousand wounded men passed over it from west to east and it still held: and towards us came train after train going from east to west – a whole corps, the XV – and still the bridge held. We felt safe at last; and we were.

Slowly, very slowly, and with long halts, we rolled on, and our supply of provisions dwindled alarmingly. The Hussar couldn't talk, but he could eat! Nitschmann and I, both belonging to the III Corps, poured out stories like soap-bubbles without end; but what kept up our spirits more than all else was the wonderful pleasure of anticipation, the thought of all of the happy days awaiting us in our homes.

The next crossing found us at Liège, and we awoke the following morning on German soil, at Aix-la-Chapelle. Good German Rhineland voices all over the station, and smiling German girls brought us our morning coffee. Our bandages were renewed by volunteer Red Cross nurses: the extremely pretty girl who cut the old bandage from my arm jabbed the point of the scissors into me, and the scar of it remains by the side of the bullet-wound to this day. The Hussar got out here, and we did not regret the loss.

Then off again with the great spaces of Germany on either side of us. Never had we appreciated to the same extent our love and our pride in it, nor how beautiful it was. The towns and villages bathed in the autumn sun had no roof in pieces, not a window pane broken. The chimneys were smoking; fine strong women, keeping their home fires burning undisturbed, waved to us from the windows, and the streets were full of happy, playing children. Yes, the homeland was unharmed, untouched by the ravages of war. We had driven it away from the frontier deep into the enemy's country, and there the battle of nations would be fought out. For that we had marched, fought, bled, and buried our best: the sacrifice was justified.

And now our train was on the great bridge over which I had crossed on the way westwards with my company; and of the four singing, cheering friends then in the carriage with me I was the only survivor.

Below us, rippling silver-green in the breeze, flowed the Rhine.

Related titles published by Helion & Company

SNIPING IN FRANCE
1914–18
With Notes on the Scientific Training
of Scouts, Observers,
and Snipers

Major H. Hesketh-Prichard DSO, MC

IMPERIAL GERMAN ARMY
1914–18
Organisation, Structure, Orders-of-Battle

Hermann Cron and Duncan Rogers

*Sniping in France 1914–18: With
Notes on the Scientific Training of
Scouts, Observers, and Snipers* (Helion
Library of the Great War Volume 1)
Major H. Hesketh-Prichard
D.S.O., M.C. 144pp, 20 sketches,
11 photos. Hardback
ISBN 1 874622 47 7

*Imperial German Army 1914–18:
Organisation, Structure, Orders of Battle*
Hermann Cron
416pp. Hardback
ISBN 1 874622 70 1

A selection of forthcoming titles

Bismarck's First War: The Campaign of Schleswig and Jutland 1864
Michael Embree   ISBN 1 874622 77 9

Hitler's Last Levy. The Volkssturm 1944–45
Hans Kissel   ISBN 1 874622 51 5

SOME ADDITIONAL SERVICES FROM HELION & COMPANY

BOOKSELLERS

- over 20,000 military books available
- four 100-page catalogues issued every year
- unrivalled stock of foreign language material, particularly German

BOOKSEARCH

- free professional booksearch service; no search fees, no obligation to buy

Want to find out more? Our website is the best place to learn more about Helion & Co. It
features online book catalogues, special offers, complete information about our own books
(including features on in-print and forthcoming titles, sample extracts and reviews), a
shopping cart system and a secure server for credit card transactions, plus much more besides!

HELION & COMPANY

26 Willow Road, Solihull, West Midlands, B91 1UE, England
Tel 0121 705 3393   Fax 0121 711 4075
Website: http://www.helion.co.uk